Frederick Taylor
and the
Public Administration
Community

SUNY series in Public Administration

Peter W. Colby, Editor

FREDERICK TAYLOR
—— and the ——
PUBLIC
ADMINISTRATION
COMMUNITY

A Reevaluation

Hindy Lauer Schachter

STATE UNIVERSITY OF NEW YORK PRESS

Published by
State University of New York Press, Albany

For information, address State University of New York
Press, State University Plaza, Albany, N.Y., 12246

Library of Congress Cataloging-in-Publication Data

Schachter, Hindy Lauer.
    Frederick Taylor and the public administration community : A
reevaluation / Hindy Lauer Schachter.
        p.   cm.—(SUNY series in public administration)
    Bibliography: p.
    Includes index.
    ISBN 0-7914-0140-5.—ISBN 0-7914-0141-3 (pbk.)
    1. Public administration—History.   2. Industrial management-
-History.   3. Taylor, Frederick Winslow, 1856–1915.   I. Title.
II. Series.
JF1341.S32   1989
350'.0009—dc20   89-4642
                                                                          CIP

10   9   8   7   6   5   4   3   2   1

Once again
to
Irving and Amanda

Contents

Acknowledgments

This book indirectly results from a Frederick Taylor symposium held at the New Jersey Institute of Technology on April 16, 1986. Asked to moderate a panel on Taylorism, I rushed to read *Shop Management* and *The Principles of Scientific Management* and discovered that in their entirety these books present a picture of Taylor's ideas that is much less authoritarian than that offered in the post-World-War-II public administration literature.

My first reaction was to share democratic aspects of Taylor's work with my audience. I entered the auditorium determined to rescue Taylor's reputation. On the platform, I became convinced that an even more important mission lay in analyzing why public administration texts give only a part of what Taylor had to say, why modern writers depict him as an organizational primitive and use him as a foil for classifying later theorists. Thus, this book was born.

I want to thank the New Jersey Institute of Technology for offering me a research sabbatical in the fall of 1987 to write the book. Much of the research was done at the Frederick Winslow Taylor collection at Stevens Institute of Technology in Hoboken, New Jersey. Taylor would have appreciated Jane Hartye, associate curator of the collection. She always seemed to find the one best way to handle any request for information.

Additional research was done at the Morris Cooke collection in the Franklin Delano Roosevelt Presidential Library in Hyde Park, New York, and at the Institute of Public Administration in New York City; I thank their staffs for assistance.

Some of the material in Chapters 2 and 4 appears in "Frederick Winslow Taylor and the Idea of Worker Participation," *Administration and Society* (May 1989). I want to acknowledge the Editorial suggestions of Gary Walmsley, the journal's editor. I also want to thank my editors at SUNY Press: Peggy Gifford, Dana Foote, and Malcolm Willison, a meticulous copy editor.

Most of all I want to thank my husband, Irving, and my daughter, Amanda, for gracious support. They both know much more about Frederick Taylor than they ever dreamed possible.

Chapter 1

Substance and Reputation —————————————

    This book is a case study analysis of how the public administration discipline integrates over time a complex and controversial theorist. The focus is on selective information transmittal, the differences that emerge between a writer's intentions and ideas—as documented in that person's books, articles, and papers—and reputation, in textbooks and articles by others. The argument is that public administration's current framework of information transmission facilitates distortion and the undervaluing of early writers, particularly through their use as foils for writers who came afterwards. A new framework for understanding the discipline's past seems necessary. In this way we can rescue complex and useful turn-of-the-century substance from attempts to make it appear less intriguing than its primary sources show it to be.

    This case study centers on rescuing from his reputation the substance of the management theorist Frederick Winslow Taylor. There is no doubt about Taylor's central role in developing management as a discipline. A 1977 survey of management historians ranked him first among the discipline's historical pioneers.[1] Dwight Waldo regards his work as the most important theoretical influence on public administration.[2] Current literature regularly alludes to him in debates on personnel administration and technological change.

    Taylor's ghost hovers over the modern study of public administration. Although he has been dead for over seventy years, discussion of his work quickly degenerates into polemics. Much of the modern literature depicts him as authoritarian, equating motivation with pay incentives. This denigration, however, focuses on a narrow range of quotations or confuses his own ideas with their purported application by people he specifically repudiated.

More is at stake here than saving a dead man's reputation. The markedly partial representation of Taylor's work is hardly accidental. Scholars deliberately choose to emphasize certain quotations and omit others. The reasons behind such choices illuminate how contemporary scholars of public administration go about understanding their discipline's history. What is at stake in investigating wrongs done the thought of Frederick Taylor is ultimately an attempt to change the way the discipline understands itself. The current framework for understanding the past must rest on false premises if it consistently skews its picture of early work. The rescue mission attempted here aims to change our understanding of what type of discipline public administration is (that is, which disciplines are its kin) by changing our understanding of the past and the way we should regard disciplinary history. Such change has profound consequences for the way we socialize new practitioners and academics into our discipline, and the way we use early sources in current research.

On one level the rescue mission entails unearthing relatively unexplored sides of Taylor's writing and suggesting ways that his ideas relate to modern issues. At a more generic level it means using the information on Taylor to question the way the field views its past. Has public administration borrowed a model of understanding from the natural sciences that is inappropriate for its own unique history? Is this model responsible for distortions in the reputation of Frederick Taylor and other early theorists? Would another model of understanding lead to fewer disparities between historical substance and reputation? These are questions that the study of Taylor's reputation helps to answer.

This book has eight chapters. The first sets the stage for a historical analysis by delineating why people interested in contemporary public administration study the history of the discipline and how current pedagogy, centering on textbooks, permits a reality/reputation disparity to grow. The second chapter summarizes Taylor's dismal reputation in modern textbooks. The next three chapters analyze Taylor's work and its reception by various factions (e.g., labor, business) in his day.

The last three chapters examine how people studying public agencies have adapted Taylor's ideas. Chapter 6 explores the relatively neglected work of Morris Cooke, a Taylor disciple, who expounds a public-sector approach to management and political relations that is reasonably close to that envisioned by his mentor. Chapter 7 focuses on mainstream public administration scholarship before America's entry into World War II. Particular attention is paid to writers associated with the New York Bureau of Municipal Research and writers of early public administration textbooks.

The final chapter explores the radically new perspective on Taylor that emerges after 1947, a focus portraying scientific management in a grossly unfavorable light (for the first time in the public administration literature) and also denigrating the contributions of early municipal reform writers associated with the New York Bureau. Attention centers on factors that fostered the sudden rise of this negative view. Earlier chapters will have already shown contrasts between Taylor's work and the portrait of his contribution in contemporary textbooks. Chapters 6 and 7 have explored contrasts between the content of pre-war public administration literature indebted to Tayloristic "scientific management" and the way such books and articles are treated by modern authors. The final chapter links these discrepancies to the inappropriate nature of the framework that public administration scholars tend to use in understanding their discipline's history. The book closes with suggestions on restructuring the preparation of young scholars to equip them for dealing with historical material, figures, and insights.

Public Administration and Historical Insight

Public administration, whether viewed as a separate field or a subspecialization of political science, is a discipline that draws on many academic subjects—as well as its own resources—to understand the management of public agencies (in comparative, national, and subnational contexts) and the development and implementation of public policies. Given its multiple roots and substantive interests, it is inevitably a hybrid discipline, placed by some universities in liberal arts schools and by others in schools of management. What constitutes its precise nature—whether science, art, or applied technology—is far from settled. Although many scholars hanker to settle the question by declaring the field a science, the ambiguity of its position actually accords nicely with the ambiguous nature of the political and managerial problems with which government agency practitioners deal. The field's position mirrors that of its subject matter.

As an academic discipline, public administration is concerned with the accumulation and organization of knowledge and thus with a form of sociability. Despite a traditional picture of lonely scholars shut in their towers, researchers hardly work in isolation.

Ideas rarely spring fully clothed from the head of a single progenitor. Each succeeding generation makes use of antecedent knowledge. Shared representations are the essence of what it means to have a discipline set off from other fields of work.[3]

In any discipline, a finite set of concepts, used over a long period of time and in differing historical circumstances, eventually undergirds research. While these ideas have continuity, the most exciting are rarely static. Meaning is fluid and negotiable. Understanding yesterday's vocabulary does not automatically proceed from comprehending how a word is used today. Alexander Hamilton speaks of a "vigorous national government"[4] and so do we. But does the phrase mean the same over the distance of two centuries? The meaning of phrases depends, at least partly, on the political, social, and economic environment in which they are used. This is particularly true in an applied discipline such as public administration, where writers are often concerned with changing as well as understanding the world. Thus, social environment plays a significant role in assigning connotation to linguistic forms.

That societal currents affect the transmittal of meaning undergirds both the essentials and the problematics of studying the history of administrative thought. Familiarity with a discipline's roots develops the historical sense necessary to political study along with the ability to think critically about current definitions of problems.[5] Seeing how one's academic forebears conceptualized concepts such as responsiveness or accountability alerts scholars to a multiplicity of available perspectives for understanding these terms. It reminds them of the diversity of administrative ideals. This shakes up preconceptions engendered by limiting one's reading to current materials that may overemphasize today's "in" mode of thought. Historical study stimulates creativity by showing the origins of the public administration tradition and the paths taken from those beginnings, while suggesting other paths not taken, which modern scholars might want to explore. Historical analysis is most likely to stimulate the critical faculties when it refrains from regarding early works as less sophisticated variants of current thought and remembers that "one reads past theories, not because they are familiar . . . but because they are strange and therefore provocative."[6]

How clearly historical study illuminates the present for young scholars depends on the way they explore the early literature. The likelihood that fewer insights will emerge is abetted by the ubiquitous use of textbooks whose *raison d'être* is to combine the diverse works of many controversial, mutually contradicting theorists into a single, progressive "mythology of coherence."[7]

Textbooks are the paramount tools of education in the natural sciences because scholars in this field assume that such works can distill all that graduate students need from early research. The natural science model of disciplinary history assumes that (1) works produced at a given point in time improve on works produced before that time, and will be in their turn improved on by later works, and (2) verbal style, wit, and nuance are peripheral to meaning. Thus the historian of science, Thomas Kuhn can defend the use of textbooks in physics:

> Why, after all, should the student of physics, for example, read the works of Newton, Faraday, Einstein or Schrödinger, when everything he needs to know about these works is recapitulated in a far briefer, more precise, and more systematic form in a number of up-to-date textbooks?[8]

Whatever the validity of this assertion in physics, the social scientist cannot a priori assume that the natural science model of the history of a discipline explains the actual relationship between earlier and successive theories in administration, that the new improves on the old rather than simply repeating old concepts in novel style. A more valid model for the history of public administration scholarship may come from the arts, which stress historical diversity of styles rather than a notion of linear progress. Such a model emphasizes analyzing each work as an entity on its own rather than primarily as a cable linking a linear narrative never envisioned by the work's progenitor. It emphasizes taking meaning from style as well as content. It is the model in use, for example, when critic Lionel Trilling urges English professors to "include on an equal footing both the traditional and the new."[9]

Most major administrative theorists present their ideas in books; they often write several, approaching similar themes in somewhat different ways at various stages of their careers. In each volume, they choose format and vocabulary they believe suitable for imparting their message. A book-length manuscript allows them ample scope to include the modulation, nuance, and ambiguity that are an important part of their thought.

A research model based on scholarship in the arts would emphasize reading authors' materials to gain meaning from their style.

Having adopted a natural science model, however, public administration textbooks may cover one person's lifetime of work in a
paragraph. Such radical synopses must discard nuance, modulation,
and ambiguity. The ideas are stripped to their skeletons. Any sort of
subtle comparison between one skeleton and another would be pa-
tently impossible if the modulations are eliminated.

Chapter 8 deals at greater length with the problems of adapting the natural science model of scholarship to the history of public
administration. Since the model presupposes disciplinary progress,
its adherents need to show that the earlier writers in any subfield
are relatively primitive compared to those who come later. Here I
only stress that early works are less amenable to distortion if public administration uses the arts model of historical understanding which relies on investigating original works themselves rather
than textbook condensations. Summaries are translations; "transla-
tor/traitor" is an old apothegm.[10] Using textbooks negates the benefits of studying a discipline's history. We want students to learn
about the past to save them from being smug and provincial. Textbooks hinder this educative process by intruding the hand of
present-day convention between students and their direct encounter with historical writers. The most we can say about a popular
textbook is that it shows how a generation of teachers transmitted
understanding. Examining the shifts in textbook content over, say, a
fifty-year period, can show how a discipline's perception of itself
shifted. Students reading textbooks in 1927 and 1987 received very
different impressions about what is crucial in Frederick Taylor's
thought. The exact wording of Taylor's volumes on our library
shelves remains unchanged. Our perception of what is crucial in
them varies. For students to gain strange and therefore provocative
ideas from Taylor (or any other historical figure), they would have to
go back and read his original work.

Original Sources

This book is very much a plea for extended use of primary
sources. One problem is time: A twenty-four-hour day ensures that
most members of the public administration community will not
read widely in their discipline's history.

A second problem involves defining what we mean by
"learning from original sources." When a contemporary public administration theorist believes that a fellow scholar has misinter-
preted his or her work, the accepted practice is for the offended

theorist to ask discipline members who are interested in the subject to check for themselves the meaning in the original work. Many readers of this book probably know about Chris Argyris and Herbert Simon's heated exchange on rationality which appeared in the *Public Administration Review* in 1973.[11] Argyris opened with a summary of Simon's views on organizational rationality. Simon countered that this was a misinterpretation, adding, "Any reader curious to know what I really think can go to the pages of *Administrative Behavior, Organizations, The Shape of Automation*, or *The Sciences of the Artificial* and discover for himself."[12] Most readers almost certainly assumed that Simon gave the best advice for discovering the "real meaning" of a contemporary work.

But would this advice work if we are concerned with the meaning of works written in earlier times, in epochs where words had different connotations than we acknowledge now? The notion of access is not as clear-cut as it may at first seem. The ability to interpret historic texts presupposes some understanding of the past and the meanings that words have had in a particular context.

If language and perception did change radically in each generation, we would find all old works undecipherable. They would be to us as hieroglyphics were to the Europeans before the discovery of the Rosetta Stone. In such an extreme case of historical discontinuity, we could gain nothing by reading material from previous eras— they would simply be too foreign to yield any meaning.

Our quandary lies in determining the extent to which language and perception change over time and make it difficult to capture the meaning intended by an early writer. To what degree can we understand an author's words in the way he or she intended? To what extent can we counter a textbook rendition of an author like Taylor by saying, "I read his books. Now I know exactly what he wanted to get across." How far will the text itself take us in answering

> the essential question which we therefore confront, in studying any given text . . . what its author, in writing at the time he did write for the audience he intended to address, could in practice have been intending to communicate by the utterance of this particular utterance.[13]

Hermeneutics reminds us that each generation reinterprets the past on the basis of its own experience.[14] Understanding emerges from the material in a historical text and from the reader's own situation. Total ability to grasp a predecessor's intentions may be a chimera. But inability to recapitulate past understanding in its entirety should not obscure the possibility of coming much closer to past authors' intentions by close attention to original texts. Grappling with original sources allows modern readers to come as near to the intended meaning as is possible—while realizing that complete unveiling of any author's intention often proves elusive.

The text is the starting point. A reader is also well advised to learn something about the work's audience, its needs and concerns. Controversies emerging around a work in its own time are helpful in clarifying the issues at stake in the author's using certain phrases. A reader who has a general knowledge of a particular period's social and economic dilemmas and how these are explicated in other works of this period will learn more about the author's intentions than one who simply reads the text itself. The modern reader can never fit squarely into the early writer's shoes, but informed approach to historical material can yield new insights.

Reading original sources is the only way to confront an author's contradictions and ambiguities. That a lifetime's work produces conflicting statements is not unusual, nor does it necessarily mean the author can be charged with carelessness or lack of integrity. The reader should consider what prompted the writer to shift opinion or to choose to express ideas ambiguously. Knowing something about the environment may explain the puzzle. For example, a shift in political leadership might compel an administrative theorist to see more clearly certain aspects of public agency management that had been obscure before. Knowing something about the intended audience is useful. Styles may shift as a writer addresses different people.

Taylor is fond of spinning long narratives to elucidate management techniques. Each time he tells one of his stories in a different work, he shifts the dialogue and action somewhat.[15] One response to such inconsistencies might be to conclude that we cannot trust the specific wording in any of the versions. More insight might be gained by asking: Why does this author choose to convey abstract meaning about management principles through semifictionalized narrative? How does this stylistic decision illuminate his intended message?

Such questions will never emerge from reading a textbook where the style of the original is ignored. Yet the answers can provide a way to reinterpret Taylor.

The usefulness of reading is particularly apparent when the aim is to juxtapose a work against its place in a discipline's modern literature. When a work or works are accorded a specific interpretation in a scholarly tradition, with certain aspects emphasized so that it fits neatly into a historical continuum, textual exegesis is an appropriate method for evaluating whether the work's actual substance supports its reputation. If textbooks give only a partial and distorted image of an author's ideas, going back to original sources is the only strategy likely to initiate a fresh look at the writer's contribution. Such rescue missions are important where an early writer's current reputation influences the way a discipline views its own past. In such cases a shift in reputation can yield a change in the way modern scholars view administrative phenomena or their own methods of understanding these phenomena. The most important rescue mission is that of changing a discipline's current outlook or methodologies by modifying our understanding of its past. A search for meanings overlooked in Taylor's writing on scientific management is such a rescue mission. It has important implications for understanding the theory of knowledge that undergirds current public administration scholarship and for proposing alternative theories that might be more useful in helping the discipline assimilate early research. It provides evidence that adopting the natural science model of understanding disciplinary history leads public administration scholars to treat early theorists as foils for later writers, even where careful review of the evidence shows the early writer anticipated many of the insights credited to the newer competitor.

Chapter 2

Taylor in Textbooks —————————————————————

Contemporary public administration textbooks treat Taylor as the ideal/typical management engineer who views workers as machines and reduces all motivation to money.[1] They speak of his "man-as-machine conceptualization, replete with all its discomforting moral overtones"[2] or his "mechanistic view of the workingman,"[3] lamenting that he "sought to refine management techniques by studying how workers might become more complete extensions of machines."[4]

Much emphasis is placed on his concern with economic man, and his failure to recognize other human aspirations. He is charged with believing that each individual "sees others purely from economic considerations,"[5] which results in "the employee . . . not [being] seen as a variable personality having needs, preferences, attitudes, and commitments."[6]

The major disagreement among the books is over the extent of Taylor's economic perspective. Some assert that he was "purely"[7] or "solely"[8] interested in economic motivation. Others insist that "he did not completely neglect the behavioral side [but] felt that high wages would generally suffice."[9] One book notes that he used economic incentives because higher wages would give the workers more respect from others.[10]

A frequent gambit in textbooks and the review literature[11] is to contrast Taylor with Elton Mayo and other Hawthorne researchers who are presented as understanding that social needs can undercut the appeal to economic rewards.[12] Taylor is also compared to the more democratic Douglas McGregor[13] and to Abraham Maslow who posits a hierarchy of five human needs—physical, security, social, esteem, and self-actualization.[14] In contrast to McGregor or Maslow, Taylor is made to appear reductionistic, a comparison in accord with the natural science scholarship model where early theory is seen as more primitive than later thinking.

A literature that contrasts Taylor and Mayo/McGregor/Maslow leads to administrative analysis that dichotomizes engineering and psychological motivation approaches. The first does things to workers (as engineers do things to machines and materials). The second views workers as active beings who can participate in their own motivating. Political theorist Sheldon Wolin turns this bisection into a battle call:

> The modern manager . . . must in defense of "human values" stand ready to resist the changes proposed by the "logicians" of industrial engineering.[15]

Proscribed are work measurement, pay-for-performance, and standardization. Lauded are psychologically oriented attempts to make workplace participation more attractive.

Fear of Taylorism (mechanistic, reductionist Taylorism) leads to a distrust of innovative workplace technologies. They are seen as harbingers of evil, engineering instrumentalities more likely to yield dehumanization than increased worker participation and shared control. Automation is viewed as an attempt to systematize and standardize tasks, to deskill jobs by stripping them of conceptual content.[16] Of course, not all writers on public administration disapprove of new technologies; some see them as potentially liberating and a force for the decentralization of power.[17] Most would agree that the direction of impact depends on implementation rather than on technology itself.[18] Few analysts would dispute that a given technology might be used to enhance human skill or degrade work. But those rejecting a particular technological application are most likely to cite the impact of Taylor's work as a reason for being cautious. The most extreme manifestation of this attitude is Frederick Thayer's repudiation of systems analysis because with this modelling technique "we are being asked to return all the way to Taylorism as it first was used by that gentleman himself!"[19]

What we see here is construction of a Golden Age tradition. Once upon a time workers controlled their jobs, for they had operational knowledge no manager could match; information was their resource for power.

The Golden Age ended when Frederick Taylor taught managers how to use technology to deskill work. People's lives were diminished through task uncoupling and degradation. Workers became little more than slaves to production rationality and "slavery to rationality, even though voluntarily accepted, is perhaps more dangerous to society than one imposed by brutal overseers]"[20]

The Elusive Golden Age

A major problem with the Golden Age is an inability to give it temporal dimensions. Exactly when were workers in organizations autonomous? When did the decline into subservience begin? Writers who want to connect Taylor with work degradation have to give some evidence that workers, either during or immediately after Taylor propounded his management theories (ca. 1895–1915), lost autonomy that they had possessed. The workers most affected should be machinists and factory laborers, two employee categories with whom Taylor conducted his work experiments.

The works of three historians contradict the existence of a clear chasm between pre- and post-Taylor epochs, with autonomy on the earlier side and subservience on the later. Merritt Roe Smith's study of pre-Civil War armories labels the 1840s as the period where conformity supplanted worker individualism, as the new technologies of the day "increased regimentation of daily routines."[21] This case study suggests that loss of autonomy occurred before Taylor was born, that the workers he encountered were already laboring in a system that hampered their creativity.

Yet David Noble and Harley Shaiken, in opposing factory implementation of computer-based automatic machine tools, present a picture of twentieth-century machinists who have maintained some control over their labor. Noble argues that in the 1940s machinists still controlled the pace of their work.[22] Shaiken gives several wonderful vignettes of machinists with considerable freedom and control. In a back-alley shop in Detroit in the 1980s, for example,

> Leo ran his lathe slower than the book said and fed the machine faster than the book said. . . . The result was a perfect part. . . . No one told Leo to run the machine faster or not to lean on the toolpost—not unless they wanted to take the responsibility for a scrapped part. Leo took that responsibility and thus had considerable freedom and control over his work environment.[23]

Workers at Ford Motor Company's enormous Rouge complex talk as though they have autonomy. Diemaker Al Gardner says, "You have to make the die on your own, and since you take responsibility for it, you don't want to be pushed around." Another diemaker, Russ Leone, states flatly, "Management depends on your knowledge."[24]

Shaiken has a negative attitude towards Taylor whom he describes as trying to make "production workers as interchangeable as the parts they were producing and skilled workers as limited and controlled as the technology would allow."[25] Yet his own account of modern machine-shop labor indicates a discrepancy between the role he and so many others assign Taylor and the man's actual impact. Leo, Al, and Russ seem to have survived as autonomous craftsmen despite alleged Taylor-era deskilling of their jobs. By their own accounts, the emergence and impact of management theory did not mark a dichotomy between a world of worker initiative and one of unilateral management control.

Historical studies yield no fixed time for the Golden Age. At one extreme, Frederick Thayer argues that the last Golden Age existed about six thousand years ago, before the development of hierarchy. For Shaiken, the real battle for control is being fought now.[26] Case studies on technology and worker involvement generally have harsh words for Taylor's role, but their cumulative impact is to dispel the myth that his work created a dichotomy, with worker autonomy rampant before he wrote and skilled labor controlled and subservient afterward.

Therefore, negative assessment of Taylor must rest on his intentions rather than his impact. The evidence lies in his books and articles rather than their application. To bolster a portrait of a man intent on deskilling labor, public administration texts should quote extensively from the man's writing. Few do so. Some offer a single short quote taken out of context. For example, they may tell readers that Taylor wrote "what the workmen want . . . beyond anything else is high wages," without adding that he also says, "of more importance still is the development of each man . . . so that he may be able to do, generally speaking, the highest grade of work for which his natural abilities fit him."[27]

Other texts cite Taylor's works without giving any quotes or referring to specific page numbers. A third group fail to cite any of Taylor's publications, relying for their knowledge on secondary sources; this leaves the reader doubting whether the authors have read any of the primary work in question or whether they are simply passing on secondhand information. Ira Sharkansky's popular text, for example, paints a portrait of Taylor based largely on material taken from two earlier textbooks, summaries presented by

Etzioni and March and Simon.[28] This approach ensures that negative reputation will outlive the reality of the man's substance. So the time has come to question the view of Taylor predicated on summarizing summaries. One way to start is by questioning the Taylor/Mayo dichotomy. An adjacent strategy is to re-examine four analyses emerging from Dwight Waldo's classic exploration of the turn-of-the-century public administration literature, analyses that modern writers use to reinforce an image of Taylor and his followers as authoritarian and limited.

Dwight Waldo's Analysis

Dwight Waldo's classic, *The Administrative State*,[29] a unique analysis of the origins and thrust of pre-World War II public administration as a field of study, identifies four problems with turn-of-the-century writers who relied heavily on Taylor's work. They (1) were too eager to borrow business concepts without considering the unique needs of the public sector; (2) used efficiency as a goal rather than a strategy; (3) valued facts over ideas or paradigms; and (4) underplayed the importance of workplace democracy.

These assertions, examined at greater length in Chapters 6 and 7, accord with an image of Taylor and his followers as reductionists. In *The Administrative State* they are imbedded in a sophisticated analysis identifying the idealism and political goals of the urban reformers who supported Taylor's analysis. However, many writers have since repeated the charges without sufficient qualification, creating a portrait of turn-of-the-century administrative writings that are more naive and apolitical than careful reading of the works indicates is the case.

It is a tribute to Waldo's strengths that few subsequent authors have resifted his ground. But a greater tribute would lie in following his example by examining his assertions, as he explored earlier writings. *The Administrative State* is a product of a particular historical moment; its publication followed by a year the first appearance in the public administration literature of a Taylor/Mayo comparison invidious to the older man.[30] Besides being an important work of historical scholarship, *The Administrative State* is also an attempt to assess the past on the basis of the discipline's needs at its particular time (1948) when public administration was attempting to form itself into a discipline more similar to the natural sciences—with more emphasis on a rigorous, scientific vocabulary—rather than relying on common sense or the style of discourse of typical agency workers. At that time, critique of the early literature was novel; now, negative analysis of Taylor is so common that the need is to reread Taylor, Mayo, and the municipal-reform literature. We need to evaluate the public administration discipline to see if it is enshrining an only partial view of its past.

Reinterpretations

Reinterpretations of historical productivity studies have occurred for the 1924–1932 research program at the Hawthorne, Illinois Western Electric Plant.

Traditional interpretations of production increases in experiments at the Hawthorne, Illinois, Western Electric Plant (1924–1932) attribute the change to more attractive intergroup relations; Elton Mayo's ability to recognize the importance of social forces supposedly separates him from the mechanistic engineering technicians.[31] Several modern reinterpretations of the Hawthorne experiments have shown that methods of motivation usually associated with Taylor (e.g., economic incentives) influenced Mayo's success at Western Electric.[32] Modern reanalysis of the production records concludes that actually "the pay rate might have been the single most important variable in the test room."[33] Test room earnings were considerably higher than the Illinois state average for comparable work, and above the regular pay that participants received before the experiments began. Mayo and other Hawthorne researchers skim lightly over the Western Electric workers' increasing their take-home pay by performing well in the tests, but surely this is as plausible a motive for hard work as any other. Where pay and human relations both improve, it is difficult to see why one should accept a priori that better personal relationships were the more important variable.

Interviews in 1981 with retired Western Electric workers who had participated in the studies show that the women themselves believe money influenced their output. One woman says flatly that she worked hard because "we made more money in the test room."[34] Increased performance feedback allowed the workers to see more clearly the relationship between completing additional relays and earning wage bonuses.

Public administration texts fail to cite the economic reinterpretations although they need to be integrated into any accurate attempt to compare Taylor and Mayo. Discovering Hawthorne's pay-for-performance dimension leads one to wonder about the human aspect of Taylor's work. If the literature obscures the reasons for productivity at Hawthorne, what does it miss in summarizing Taylor's contribution?

Without trying to overcompensate and turn Taylor into a prophet of the self-managed workplace, three articles from the business management literature suggest that he was not oblivious to social relations, that he had an innate concern with improving worker participation. He believed that his ideas would succeed because they improved an organization's social climate and enhanced labor's ability to meet diverse needs.

Peter Drucker argues that Taylor's motivational strategies provided the worker with an opportunity for full personality development.[35] Louis Fry asserts that most negative assessments of Taylor's work come from evaluating practice in factories claiming to follow his methods rather than close reading of his own works.[36] (This method of assessment would only be valid if we were concerned with impact rather than intention. The present rescue mission focuses on intentions as developed in Taylor's works.) Edwin Locke surveys some critiques of Taylor's work and concludes that "Taylor has never been fully understood or appreciated by his critics. . . . His major ideas and contributions often have gone unacknowledged."[37]

None of these writers argue that Taylor was not concerned with economic motivation or that he did not share some of the managerial prejudices of his day. Modern writers who narrowly characterize Taylor bolster their portrait with accurate quotes—but these quotations are a miniscule fraction of Taylor's output. Side by side with his few condescending or authoritarian pronouncements are many paragraphs anticipating human relations strategies that most public-administration textbooks attribute to later authors.

Taylor's modern defenders have not yet offered a substantial analysis of his work to show rather than tell readers his actual orientation. That task falls to this book. The following two chapters integrate analysis of Taylor's whole body of writing with information on his personal and social background. They do not provide a detailed biography, which is available elsewhere.[38] Chapter 3 sketches the labor milieu of the 1870s and 1880s when Taylor encountered the factory. It analyzes the conditions he set out to reform and the changes he proposed in the way managers approached motivation. Both chapters examine the audience he intended to reach and how this affected his writing style—which words to use, where to place emphasis, when to introduce semific-tional narratives. Taylor uses words and metaphors he believes appropriate to people working on a factory floor. The seventh chapter presents the argument that his stylistic decisions (which the public administration textbooks ignore) indicate the inherently democratic message his works impart. His ultimate meaning would be different if he had adopted the more technical, scientific vocabulary of the Hawthorne researchers. I shall attempt to show that use of the model of scholarship in the arts would highlight this particular difference between Taylor and Mayo.

Chapter 3

Early Years ——————————————————————————————

Frederick Winslow Taylor was born to an affluent Philadelphia family in 1856. His father, Franklin, was an 1840 Princeton University graduate who worked for several years as a lawyer before retiring to live on ample stock and real-estate assets. His mother, Emily Winslow, was a member of a prominent Quaker family.

Frederick's early background mingled aristocratic and capitalist values. His father's decision to leave work represents stereotypical European gentry values rather than those of the hustle bustle, of the make-more-while-you-can American world. The Taylor parents insisted that their children learn classical languages although Frederick preferred doing experiments and watching animals. Fred had two years of schooling in France and Germany and one and a half years of European travel, of which he wrote later, "I disapprove for a young boy."[1]

At the same time the family participated in several institutions and movements concerned with modern values such as rationality and equality. Franklin and Emily left the Quaker faith to join the Unitarian community, which emphasized tolerance of differences in religious opinion. Emily was an outspoken abolitionist attacked before the Civil War as anti-American for attending an anti-slavery conference in London; she was a feminist who worked with Lucretia Mott.

In 1872, Fred entered the Phillips Exeter Academy. After a mediocre first term, he moved to the head of his class, doing particularly well in mathematics. In 1874 he passed Harvard University's entrance examination. He now appeared ready to follow his father's footsteps—graduate from an Ivy League school and become a lawyer. But such continuity was shattered when Fred complained of headaches and vision problems, which he attributed to heavy studying. He convinced his parents that his health required that he forego the opportunity to enter Harvard. The life for him was one of manual labor. In the fall of 1874, he became an apprentice machinist at Philadelphia's Enterprise Hydraulic Works.

Although Taylor's official biographer takes the eye-strain story at face value,[2] the sudden shift from Harvard to manual labor bears scrutiny. Nothing in Taylor's background propelled the choice. Franklin subscribed to a gentry ethic that stressed cultivated leisure rather than the moral value of work. A son with a vision problem would be welcome to loll temporarily at home, go to concerts, travel in America or Europe. Even if his headaches precluded Harvard, they did not impel him to a factory. The choice of spending long days at Enterprise Hydraulic represents a strange way for someone in Fred's economic position to cure a vision ailment.

Harley Shaiken describes a modern machine shop in terms that make it seem an unlikely sanctuary from headaches and eye problems:

> You notice it is noisy. Metal is being ground, sawed, hammered, bent and cut; compressed air is blowing chips out of the path of cutters; heavy machine motors are in gear. It is smelly. . . . By the standards of the office, it is dirty. Metal filings and long, curled steel chips are scattered over the machines, workbenches and floor.[3]

In the 1870s factory conditions were even less salubrious. Work was done in hot, dirty, poorly lighted rooms.[4] Pattern making, an integral part of Taylor's apprenticeship, required close eye work in learning to read complicated mechanical drawings.

The only plausible explanation for the whole caper is that Fred preferred being a machinist to a college student. Most Americans of that era never faced the choice between academic or factory labor; economic circumstances forced the latter alternative on most of them. Fred was almost certainly the only Enterprise apprentice to choose that berth over four student years at a respected Ivy League university. He was in a machine shop from intellectual choice rather than necessity.

It is crucial to realize that the young Taylor enjoyed manual labor; he recognized machine shop work as important and interesting, not only something a smart person might want to write about but something he himself would want to do on a daily basis. Years later, Taylor reminisced about his apprenticeship, saying, "I there learned appreciation, respect and admiration for the everyday working mechanic."[5] But had he not already had such appreciation before he entered the hydraulic works, he would never have used a factory as a respite from Harvard.

Some of this attitude stayed with him all his life. Immediately after completing his apprenticeship in 1878, he saw that the lack of a baccalaureate might prove a career disadvantage. Although his parents' financial circumstances permitted him to resume full-time studies at any university, he ruled out leaving the shop floor. He spent time searching for a technical college that would allow him to get a degree while working full time. We will probably never know whether Stevens Institute of Technology in Hoboken, New Jersey, was the only school that allowed him to gain a degree by simply passing its entrance and final examinations. We do know that Taylor accepted this arrangement and received a Stevens bachelor of science in mechanical engineering in 1883 without attending classes.

Thirty-five years after starting at Enterprise Hydraulic, Taylor, in a lecture to the Society for the Promotion of Engineering Education, urged all college students (even those in classics or theology) to spend a year between their freshman and sophomore years working in a factory. There, he said, they would learn that lathe operators were their equals. They would see that the work machinists did required a fund of knowledge equally important as that required in the traditional professions.[6]

The apprentice Taylor straddled two worlds. He was an Exeter graduate from a prominent family; by birth and education, he was a member of the managerial class, not simply another anonymous hand. As he noted many years later, "My father had some means and owing to the fact that I worked during my first year of apprenticeship for nothing . . . I was given . . . special opportunities to progress from one kind of work to another."[7]

Yet he was still an apprentice. He did manual labor, and got dirt and oil on his clothes. Scientific management is a product of both Taylor's background and his experience applied to the concerns of his time. His writing reacts against administrative shortcomings he first saw at Enterprise and at the Midvale Steel Company where he became a journeyman in 1878. Since the tenor of factory life in the 1870s and 1880s constitutes the foundation for his proposals for administrative reform, understanding Taylor's work requires some knowledge of the factory hierarchy and decision making he encountered. The following section summarizes managerial control patterns of the period; we then examine Taylor's reaction to them.

The Factory Milieu

Decentralized production decision making was the norm in late-nineteenth-century factories. Foremen had substantial influence in determining schedules and the cost and quality of output.[8] In some companies, foremen were virtually internal contractors. Top managers gave them almost unlimited control over employees, including the right to hire, set and reduce wages, and terminate at will. Captain Henry Metcalfe, chief of the Frankford Arsenal in the 1880s, called a foreman "the head of all the men, the acknowledged brains ruling the motions of a hundred hands."[9] Ernest Brown, who worked at Acme Wire Company before 1904, labelled this organization "the old-fashioned 'foreman do it all' type."[10]

This loose, decoupled system extended to individual skilled workers. On a day-to-day basis each was free to use his own tools and work methods. Central management determined what the factory produced; supervisors structured the production process; craft workers chose motions and tools to complete a particular object.

This shop-floor decentralization is celebrated in the Golden Age literature, where it is seen as a precursor of our own "job enrichment."[11] A very different attitude prevailed in the American management literature written between 1870 and 1900.[12] Taking a top-down perspective, these writers decry the system's lack of coordination and continuity. Problems associated with foreman control include: lost orders, kept only in a foreman's head; duplicated work; instability from foreman succession since without centralized rules and procedures a foreman leaving takes all of his knowledge from the company.

A bottom-up view also shows the system's flaws. Decentralization was a recipe for anxiety from supervisors' having almost unlimited power to hire and fire their subordinates. Managers could terminate foremen, or change their rate of pay, without giving any justification; foremen possessed similar power over their workers. Every factory employee knew that he or she had to please those placed above; all knew that brute survival meant meeting a supervisor's expectations. A lack of well-defined, centrally accepted written procedures simply meant that workers received no preparation, no blueprint to help them succeed.

Two examples illustrate the problem. A volume of turn-of-the-century manager-foreman communications from the Dwight Manufacturing Company has been examined by Daniel Nelson.[13] The prevalent mode for managers to show displeasure was to tell a foreman to improve or face dismissal. No detailed performance appraisals or suggestions on how to improve were considered necessary. Hiring and firing substituted for training or performance feedback provision. True, foremen were left to guide their own actions; was this a source of foremen's psychic ease, particularly for those who were slow to develop in one particular area? Was it not rather a source of their anxiety?

The problem was more acute for entry-level workers. A group of men who had worked in nineteenth-century Milwaukee factories were interviewed in the 1950s about their supervisors.[14] They produced a picture of foremen who rarely trained slow workers, of a job that simply did not include pointing out mistakes and offering corrections. The response to an unsatisfactory worker was to utter a few curses and dismiss him. Like foremen themselves, ground-level employees suffered from a lack of early feedback and development.

A typical foreman received his position by rising through the organization's ranks. He was comfortable with the plant's work routines but not necessarily with teaching techniques or any motivational strategies. Some foremen bolstered their authority with physical compulsion. Harlow Person recalled that as a factory worker in the 1890s, he saw that "management's concept of a proper day's work was what a foreman could *drive* workers to do."[15] As late as 1912, steel-industry foremen were known as "pushers" because they physically propelled their gangs.[16]

The threat behind this system appears clearly in some remarks made by a Brooklyn manager, John Hawkins, who, in trying to defend the lack of instruction, explained how he motivated workers when he entered a new plant in 1877:

> I did not know a single one of the workmen in the whole concern, but I called them together and I talked to them just as an employer or superintendent should talk to a number of men. . . . I gave them to understand that if they did the best they could, due consideration would be given them; and a dismissal or reduction of pay to those who did the worst. In the course of two or three weeks I found it necessary to discharge half a dozen men. . . . I discharged them as examples, and I

found my actions resulted in great improvement on the part of the rest of the men.[17]

This manager used dismissal as a training device, *pour encourager les autres*. Instead of teaching workers the nature of the methods he considered useful, Hawkins, like many other managers of his time, left employees free to learn "the best" or face the fate of the discharged half a dozen.

The 1870s and 1880s hardly constitute a Golden Age in factory relations. The system's arbitrary nature led to deep-seated labor/management animosity. This is an era of strikes and lockouts and boycotts and the infamous Haymarket affair where the Knights of Labor's attempt to hold a general strike frightened the Chicago middle class and led to violence.[18] Less dramatically, it was a time when workers responded to the precariousness of their situation by informally sharing whatever indefinite oral information they possessed on factory standards, including, in some instances, the minimum they could accomplish and still expect to keep their jobs. Faced with hourly pay scales, no training and relatively few promotion opportunities, they had neither career nor economic incentives for maximizing productivity. It is reasonable to assume that some responded by trying to ascertain "how little they could do and hold their jobs."[19] Taylor's writings are a reaction against these shortcomings of the decoupled system.

Taylor and the Factory Milieu

From 1878 to 1890 Taylor worked at the Midvale Steel Company in Philadelphia. He entered the firm as a machine-shop journeyman and left as chief plant engineer. With his first promotion to foreman or gang boss, his official duties involved overseeing day-by-day production. According to his own account, his approach to managing people was conventional for his era. His first instinct was simply to copy the patterns set by other foremen and try to raise output by driving. He demanded that his machinists work more quickly. They banded together to resist the new autocrat just as they had resisted other foremen in the past. He later recalled:

> As soon as I became gang boss the men who were working under me and who, of course, knew that I was onto the whole game of soldiering or deliberately restricting output, came to me at once and said, "Now, Fred, you are not going to be a

damn piece-work hog, are you?" I said, "If you fellows mean you are afraid I am going to try to get a larger output from these lathes," I said, "Yes; I do propose to get more work out." I said, "You must remember I have been square with you fellows up to now and worked with you. I have not broken a single rate. I have been on your side of the fence. But now I have accepted a job under the management of this company and I am on the other side of the fence, and I will tell you frankly that I am going to try to get a bigger output from those lathes."[20]

When production failed to rise, he fired some men and lowered others' wages—standard 1870s operating procedure. As he believed some of the workers retaliated by breaking machine parts or damaging goods, he fined those responsible.

After some two years of internecine warfare, Taylor tried to increase productivity by teaching the machinist's trade to unskilled laborers. In return, he asked them to run the lathes at his suggested speed. Of course the unskilled workers promised to comply—this was almost certainly their only chance at a career boost. Trained and at their posts, they absorbed the crew's norms and soon came down to the old output that Taylor found unsatisfactory.

Years later, Taylor remembered how angry he became during this battle.[21] But at some point, his background helped give him the breadth of vision to step out of the constraints of his foreman's role to realize that the factory system itself rather than the workers might bear the blame for his problems. Insufficient information interfered with any chance to increase production. He wanted machinists to match his notion of a fair day's work, but where was the evidence that his assumptions coincided with reality? As a foreman he needed more information on the dimensions of a fair day's work before he could offer a reasonable challenge.

He noted:

> When I came to think over the whole matter, I realized that the thing which we on the management's side lacked more than anything else was exact knowledge as to how long it ought to take the workman to do his work. . . . I could take any workman and show him how to run his lathe, but when it came to telling a man how long it ought to take him to do his work there was no foreman who at that time could do this with any degree of accuracy.[22]

In other words, the foreman could fire workers whom he thought were moving too slowly—even though no one had an accurate estimate of what a fair day's work might be.

The machinists, on the other hand, needed information on how productivity improvement would be in their interest. The struggle over work norms at Midvale convinced Taylor that forcing people to go against their interests was futile. He learned how difficult it is to tell workers "do so much X" unless you are prepared to show how "X" is done and how its maximum accomplishment benefits the people who exert the effort. The workers could be fired for working too slowly, but managers raised piece work rates at will, and labor had no guarantee that working more quickly than the norm would bring any economic gain to them. Taylor admitted

> after my first fighting blood which was stirred up through strenuous opposition had subsided, I did not have any bitterness against any particular man or men. My anger and hard feelings were stirred up against the system.[23]

By the mid-1880s Taylor was attempting to increase the information available to managers and workers on the concept of a fair day's work and its incentives, first by determining the approximate time workers needed to produce specific items. With a stopwatch, he timed labor, recording motions and lapsed intervals. This information allowed him to experimentally shift equipment or tool size to see if these transitions changed the time required to complete a given job.[24] He also supplemented oral directives (the prevalent foreman/crew mode of communication) with written cards and bulletin boards.

At some point, his persona shifted from an operating engineer, primarily employed to supervise work in a particular plant, to a researcher, trying to construct a science of work. Experiments occupied an increasing part of his work day. He hired Henry Gantt, a fellow Stevens graduate, and Carl Barth, a Norwegian draftsman, to assist in the time and motion studies. He read at least some of the burgeoning management literature of his time. In 1886 he joined the American Society of Mechanical Engineers (ASME) at the very time that the organization (founded in 1880 at Stevens Institute of Technology) was beginning to include presentations on management. At his first national conference, the association's vice president called for greater attention to record keeping and the flow of internal information.[25] Although public administration textbooks often portray Taylor as authoritarian, his true loyalty was always to his ideas rather than to this or that hierarchy. Many of his superiors considered the notion of a science of work as alien. He can be accused of "soldiering" himself for using so much of his Midvale time on his experiments, a lapse for which he was at least once reprimanded.

In 1890 he left Midvale to take his last line position, as general manager of a paper products firm, the Manufacturing Investment Company. Three years later he decided to become a consulting management engineer. In the next eight years his clients included Simmonds Rolling Machine Company (Fitchburg, Massachusetts), Cramps Ship and Engine Building Company (Philadelphia), Northern Electrical Manufacturing Company (Cleveland), Johnson Company (Chicago), and Bethlehem Steel Company (Bethlehem, Pennsylvania), for which he did the consulting work on pig iron loading and shoveling that figures in his later books.

Throughout this period Taylor pursued the strategy of using experimentation to ascertain which tools and operating procedures gave maximum output. Rather than accepting a given machine shop's work practices, he asked what would happen if he changed the tool shape, the quality or hardness of the metal being cut, the depth of the cut, or the thickness of the feed or shaving?

He was willing to work long hours on a single problem, finding improvements for a tool and then returning to a lathe to see what further refinements might make the implement even more useful. He defined his credo:

> The true experimenter must be an enthusiast; he should have the keen delight in obtaining a result that the ordinary man would have in finding a diamond mine. This very enthusiasm, however, leads most experimenters into perhaps their worst error or fault, namely a desire to always get a positive, useful result, whereas perhaps nine out of ten experiments when truthfully carried out must lead to negative results. . . . The true experimenter sets no time limit, but is willing to look forward for years and plod away.[26]

Taylor was headstrong enough to see experimentation almost as combat. Yet he did not rely for knowledge only on his own studies; he was alert to the management concerns of others he encountered at the meetings of the American Society of Mechanical Engineers (ASME).

Taylor and Systematic Management

Foremen's specific difficulties were the immediate cause of Taylor's Midvale experiments, yet production imbroglios were unique neither to Midvale nor the steel industry. As Taylor fought his early, misguided battles with his workers, other engineer/managers experienced their own production problems and tried to formulate general rules to help them and their successors not repeat past mistakes.

An administrative historian notes that the 1880s can be seen as "the decade in which the budding, if not full flowering of administrative thought took place in terms recognizable today."[27] Engineer/managers embraced the rather novel idea that practitioners could improve their performance by systematically evaluating problems and options and choosing methods that alleviated some of the causes for concern (e.g., confronting a problem of duplicated orders, evaluating options and choosing a solution, such as standardized written order forms). The issues Taylor tackled were similar to some of the concerns of senior writers in the field, and his initiatives responded, to some extent, to their formulas as well as day-by-day Midvale and consulting realities.

Two major areas in this literature were techniques for distributing information and for using wage incentives. Although Taylor's ideas in both these fields eventually outran those of the writers he read and argued with at ASME meetings, he admitted that his efforts to increase information flow matured through "slow evolution" and "gradual development," and benefited from contact with the "complete, well thought out invention . . . of Captain [Henry] Metcalfe,"[28] the originator of the written order card. The following two sections examine Taylor's contact with Metcalfe and with ASME writers who were exploring new wage incentives.

Henry Metcalfe

Captain Henry Metcalfe, of the United States Army Ordnance Department, was in charge of the gun-making workshops at Frankford Arsenal, a position that involved the need to increase productivity (which was considered low in arsenals)[29] and manage people. While Taylor was engaged in his early Midvale battles, Metcalfe had progressed enough to write *The Cost of Manufactures*, publicly broaching the need for an administrative science whose researchers would collect and classify past records to produce generic principles to apply in future cases.

Metcalfe had a fairly sophisticated grasp of the philosophical difficulties inherent in creating such a science. He noted that researchers might inadvertently distort evidence because of personal bias, and suggested having several people work together to minimize this problem.[30] He reflected on the great diversity in organizations, which might vitiate the extent to which one group of structural or decision-making improvements could actually help all managers. He was almost unique in his era for noting that public agencies might need different administrative structures than businesses did. At a time when Woodrow Wilson could write that public administration was simply another business field,[31] Metcalfe argued that public factories had dual characteristics: Like private firms, they needed efficient methods, but unlike businesses they had to face legislative accountability, even if this diminished their efficiency.[32] An arsenal manager had to be careful to differentiate which private organizations' methods were applicable to his operations.

Like Taylor, Metcalfe was concerned with the inadequate flow of information in production units. Taylor's search was more multidimensional, for he wanted to increase two types of flow—both that concerning actual conditions (through cards and bulletin boards) and possibilities (through time and motion studies). Metcalfe's purview was narrower: For him, information meant readily available data on the actual situation (e.g., number of orders or pieces completed), rather than what ought to happen (Taylor's concept of a fair day's work).

The problem Metcalfe confronted was that the decoupled system left each foreman free to keep whatever records he chose, if any. As production supervisors, most foremen considered information exchange a secondary concern at best; they kept meager records on work pending and completed. Metcalfe made an early appeal for specialization by advocating that companies remove record keeping from the foreman's list of duties and instead hire clerks whose job would center on communicating information.

Taylor met Metcalfe at the 1886 meeting of the ASME, an organization that provided a congenial home to practicing engineers who wanted to generalize about management problems.[33] The captain's paper dealt with increasing written communications and hiring clerks, as strategies to expedite the flow of organizational information.[34] During the discussion period, Taylor offered his first public pronouncement on management, commenting that he too was trying to increase information flow, that he used order cards and written instructions. At this point, Taylor was obviously the neophyte. Metcalfe's more highly developed strategy permitted two-way communication with the workers who were writing cards detailing what they had done; Taylor at that time relied on top-down written communication only. The interaction with Metcalfe may have prompted him towards a clearer view of the possibilities inherent in changing organizational practices; the possible scope of change may have seemed wider after Taylor learned of the arsenal innovations.

The exchange is important for two additional reasons. First, it underscores the central role that getting adequate information on actual conditions played at the time; neither Taylor nor anyone else refers to the more radical notion of ascertaining possibilities. (Although Taylor was already working on time and motion studies, he does not mention them in the recorded discussion.) Second, for students of public administration, the exchange highlights the close ties between the engineer/managers of the 1880s and Captain Metcalfe, who argued for public/private sector distinctions. Most modern public administration scholars associate the 1880s with Woodrow Wilson's equation of public and business management, and consider the discovery of unique public-sector goals and strategies a modern improvement. In actuality, nineteenth- and early-twentieth-century engineers who wrote about public management were much more familiar with Metcalfe's work than Wilson's. Contrary to the implication of most public administration textbooks, the engineering management tradition starts from the argument that public/private differences exist and that efficiency may not always be the single most important goal in the public sector. This point will be developed in later chapters.

Wage Incentives

Between 1886 and 1895, wage administration constituted the primary management issue discussed at ASME meetings, Metcalfe's being the only substantive management paper that does not focus on it. These meetings brought Taylor in contact with a burgeoning literature on bonuses, a literature that in some respects still has relevance to modern debates on merit pay.

These papers expostulated against the widely prevalent nineteenth-century practice of wage reductions. William Partridge identified the underlying problem in an 1887 ASME paper on "Capital's Need for High-Priced Labor."[35] He argued that pay incentives were worse than useless as motivators because factory owners prized low wages regardless of worker output. Assume a factory where the high wage for labor is $10 per week. The foremen introduce a piece work system. Skilled workers soon perform so well that they are earning $20 a week. Rather than proffering congratulations, the owners are likely to fret over "high" wages and cut the base piece rate until no one earns more than the original $10. Soon workers learn not to increase production at the start of a piece work system because eventually the bosses penalize strong performance. Owners will not allow workers to share the monetary rewards of higher productivity.

While Partridge's paper deals solely with economic motivation, he is hardly arguing that money alone motivates. He makes the very different—almost self evident—point that a wage system cannot serve a motivating function as long as workers have reason to fear base pay reductions. To the extent that money rewards might improve performance, owners have to change their wage practices to improve productivity.

Within a year, Henry Towne, the president of the Yale and Towne Manufacturing Company, outlined a prototype incentive plan designed without any base pay reductions.[36] Called "gain sharing," this scheme depended on recording a job's traditional cost and assigning all the workers involved on that job a predetermined bonus based on how much money they saved from the traditional cost. Towne argued that owners would use this plan without instituting wage cuts as long as the bonus was kept small enough so that it did not upset management's profit from the more intensive labor.

In 1891, Frank Halsey attacked Towne's plan for rewarding more productive and less productive workers equally since everyone assigned to a job received the same predetermined bonus for overall increases in productivity.[37] Halsey offered instead a "premium plan" based on recording each worker's traditional job time and apportioning premiums for each hour a worker saved on his own. (Productive workers would receive bonuses; slower or more careless ones would not.) Halsey argued that the keystone of his system lay in keeping premiums less than a worker's hourly base wage. Since a worker cutting an hour off his time did not receive an extra hour's pay but rather something less than half that, the arrangement should be palatable to owners.

At the June 1895 meeting in Detroit, Taylor joined the fray with a paper amalgamating the prevalent concern for usable incentives with a critique of both Towne and Halsey based on his own insights from the Midvale experiments. We have no way of knowing exactly how much of his proposal stemmed from hearing earlier presentations, how much came from his experience at work with everyday wage reductions. Towne seems close to the mark when he speculated,

> I have no reason whatever to believe that Taylor's work was prompted by anything which I did or wrote, although there appears to be some ground for the belief that my paper may have awakened him to a realization of the significance of his own work.[38]

The Towne and Halsey proposals conflicted with Taylor's emphasis on experimenting to learn better ways to do work. He joined the debate in 1895, at least in part, to underscore the unreliability of any pay incentive scheme based on insufficient information on what constituted a fair day's work. He argued, in effect, that Towne and Halsey both had placed the cart before the horse in devising numerical pay tactics before they had information on worker capabilities.

Taylor opened his career as a management theorist at the 1895 ASME meeting in somewhat prophetic style by condemning late nineteenth-century rate reductions as "evil." Business needs pay policies to unite employee and manager interests; instead, owners present a rate reduction system likely to create "a permanent antagonism between employers and men."[39]

Which pay policies are likely to increase production without demoralizing workers? An hourly wage would not by itself increase performance. A reasonable base rate and a chance to increase earnings through effort are a necessary (if insufficient) condition for eliciting or rewarding a desire to perform more efficiently.

The argument is not that wages alone motivate. The 1895 paper is subtitled "a Step toward Partial Solution of the Labor Problem," and its author is well aware that wages constitute only one facet in motivation. While Towne and Halsey limit their discussions to economic motivation, Taylor notes (if in passing) that promotions from within and good personal relations are also important influences, and that some workers are so demoralized by past treatment that no incentives can make them care. A reasonable wage system is not the only or all-powerful panacea but it is a necessary foundation after the "demoralizing effect"[40] of the present system. As Abraham Maslow would argue many years later, basic needs must be satisfied before higher needs come into play.[41]

By focusing on wages, Taylor followed a line of thought established by earlier analysts. The principal breakthrough lies in his critique of the Towne and Halsey proposals, which were both predicated on using only current output to set base rates. Their gain-sharing and premium plans are based on the assumption that current practice approximates a fair day's work. Taylor asks, why accept this assumption?

An equitable system requires solid information. Researchers have to break jobs into constituent operations and determine the time each requires under various circumstances. Such studies supply empirical evidence on how long jobs take using different technologies. Once all the people involved know the most appropriate equipment and work styles, managers can institute a piece rate system that is fair to both the owners and the workers, with a higher rate for jobs done quickly and well, and a lower rate for work that takes longer or is of poor quality.

For the system to work, the people on the factory floor need training in how to use tools in ways to improve productivity; they require frequent feedback to know how they are doing and how they can improve each day. Although this breaks with nineteenth-century sink-or-swim practice, Taylor defended how essential training and feedback were in a system where research would yield calculation of productive methods that could be shared with the workers as a form of employee development. He argues that workers even prefer negative feedback rather than having a supervisor pass by in silence day after day as if they were machines. The sensible manager uses the feedback sessions as an opportunity to hear the worker point of view as well as giving his own. This requires good human relations because,

> the employer who goes through his works with kid gloves on, and is never known to dirty his hands or clothes, and who either talks to his men in a condescending or patronizing way, or else not at all, has no chance whatever of ascertaining their real thoughts or feelings.[42]

The 1895 paper proffers a more balanced approach to labor-management conflict than those provided by Towne or Halsey. Earlier presentations assumed that the only change needed to increase productivity is greater worker motivation. Taylor was the first to point out that indolence and indifference affect managers too. Part of the problem emerges from managerial refusal to take the time and trouble to investigate better work technologies and train labor.

Ironically, the man whom modern textbooks depict as reso-
lutely pro-management ends his first paper with the prediction that
few companies would adopt his ideas because it is managers who
want to stay with their accustomed strategies. He is more sanguine
about workers' accepting the new system for gains to themselves as
individuals and about the power of the work group to spur its
members to work harder so all may get higher pay.

Spirited debate followed the presentation. Exchanges occurred
both at the meeting where the paper itself was given and at subsequent national ASME conferences when the ideas were raised and
rehashed over and over again. Some listeners responded with hor-
ror stories of rate cuts in their factories where "men were trying to
do their best, but by doing their best they were compelled to work
harder and were getting less and less pay."[43] But the prevalent reaction, in one observer's view, was universal dissent from all participants aged over fifty.[44]

The tenor of the objections did not come from the direction
one might expect after reading modern public administration textbooks. No one at the meeting criticized Taylor for taking power
away from workers—or praised him for giving control to managers.
To talk of taking labor power away would have been absurd after
listening to a discussant speak of employees who worked very hard
to meet a contract to drive 2,500 rivets, only to be told by the boss
that if they could do 2,500, he would require 3,500 next time at a
lower rate![45]

The objections raised would be difficult, in the main, for modern readers to understand. One faction defended the ongoing system, alleging that the problem lay in new workers' lack of moral
fiber rather than in an unmet need for incentives or training. One
manager who took this point of view argued that the solution to
low productivity was to,

> induce every man who enters a shop to work to do the best
> that is in him for the wages he has agreed to receive—which
> was generally the fashion when I was a young man—instead
> of doing the least possible, as is now the prevailing style.[46]

Another group criticized the plan because it gave labor too
much money. Frank Halsey wondered why the workers deserved
any bonus at all if management performed the experiments and
sponsored the training sessions.[47] At any rate, large bonuses were a
form of overkill because "a comparatively small premium will call

out a workman's best efforts, provided the work is not too laborious and the workman is *assured against future cuts.*"[48]

In defending his own premium plan, Halsey also made a more prescient objection. He questioned the possibility of actually establishing a work science. His own system, hinging on the use of current rates, might not reflect a fair day's work in all circumstances, but the use of actual production figures saved managers from the "danger of expensive errors of judgment." Taylor's ideas might sound more innovative, but Halsey contended, "it is hard to conceive anything so simple or safe as the plan offered by me."[49]

Taylor was sorry about the reception his paper received, particularly since only Halsey commented on the idea that Taylor considered the crux of his system—gathering information on a fair day's work by performing work experiments. Most of the discussion centered on size of bonuses and other points Taylor believed peripheral, not the heart of his unique contribution. Halsey challenged Taylor to produce a longer paper that would supply details on how to conduct work experiments and explain how managers could gather information that would yield performance improvements the ASME audience could use to gauge the usefulness of the new plan.

Eight years elapsed before Taylor obliged. These years were occupied with the consulting work that provided empirical examples and narratives to bolster an emerging model of management and motivation. Stress pervaded this period as Taylor experienced his first taste of working for entrepreneurs who wanted his services while not necessarily accepting all of his ideas (e.g., a manager might want to install a bonus system but not install adequate training or feedback).

Taylor's approach to management reform hinged on a company's allowing him time to perform work experiments that would yield more proficient tool design and operating procedures before expecting to reap financial rewards through greater productivity. Strife occurred if Taylor believed that line managers wanted to take shortcuts that afforded speedier fiscal gains while providing less accurate information on work and less chance of bequeathing a useful operating system in the long run. Taylor's official biographer notes that the man's idealistic instinct was to ask, "What ought we to have?", and to object if line managers responded with, "What can we do with what we have or can get quickly?"[50] A more recent analysis argues that this propensity to idealize and disregard the conflict his presence caused stemmed from Taylor's personal struggle to accept discipline and authority.[51]

Relations with Robert Linderman, Bethlehem Steel's financier president, were particularly stormy. The men clashed over Taylor's request for higher salaries for works officers and over use of new accounting methods. Linderman dismissed him as a consultant on May 1, 1901. A letter Taylor wrote to a friend shows how petulant he could be when he thought an executive did not accept the need for adequate preparation:

> Personally my experience has been so unsatisfactory with financiers that I never want to work for any of them. . . . As a rule, financiers are looking merely for a turnover. It is all a question of making money quickly and whether the company is built up so as to be the finest of its kind and permanently successful is a matter of complete indifference.[52]

Frederick Taylor had the financial wherewithal to place allegiance to ideas over acceptance of half-way measures. Eight years of consulting had sharpened his perspective on the requirements for effective management and the impediments awaiting any fundamental proposal for change. The Bethlehem debacle prodded him to retire from active practice and devote his energies to codifying and promoting the ideas that he described as alternately a new art or a new science of management, a discipline that he explicitly presented as based on good employer/employee relations.[53]

He wrote as an outsider, a man whose birth and education precluded his ever being one with the workers, but a person who understood (at least after Bethlehem) that his vision was not that of the typical line manager, either. Critiquing organizations from the outside gave him the ability to take a long-term perspective; but it also meant that he could never implement his own plans on his own, he could only suggest innovations. Turning theory into practice rested on others' shoulders, a source of contention throughout his lifetime, and afterwards.

Chapter 4

Scientific Management ————————————————————

Shop Management and *The Principles of Scientific Management* are the two works that embody Taylor's mature ideas on organizational improvement and motivation.[1] Although the first originated as a 1903 ASME presentation[2] and the second was originally serialized in the April, May, and June, 1911 *American Magazine* (circulation 340,000), they can be examined as a single entity. Taylor wrote them for the same audience, chiefly industrial managers and engineers; their arguments are similar to the extent that the author quotes chunks of *Shop Management* in the later *Principles*.

A third published source for Taylor's ideas is his January 1912 testimony before a special House of Representatives committee convened to investigate the social impact of shop management systems.[3] This is a particularly valuable source for people who want to understand how Taylor envisioned management principles, since here he replies to criticisms of the earlier presentations.

The next two chapters present a picture of scientific management from the works themselves. Chapter four describes the central proposals advanced in *Shop Management* and *Principles*. Chapter five analyzes how adherents and opponents reacted to these proposals. It discusses Taylor's rebuttal, including his attempt to separate his ideas from their application by others more attuned to his new mechanisms of management rather than to his underlying ideals. It also explores the problem of Taylor's idealism.

Shop Management

For Taylor, management, alternately described as an art and as a science, is essentially a question of the relations between employers and employees. What is wanted is a system that gives satisfaction to both, shows that their best interests are mutual and can "bring about such thorough and hearty cooperation that they can pull together instead of apart."[4]

Historically, Taylor argues, such cooperation has been impossible because employers, ignorant of actual work time and indifferent to individual workers, have equated low wages with the low labor costs they desired, to the point that,

> it is safe to say that the majority of employers have a feeling of satisfaction when their workmen are receiving lower wages than those of their competitors.[5]

This attitude defeats any chance to increase productivity because employees, seeing that hard work brings no monetary reward, adopt a slow pace, marking time or "soldiering." The end result is loss to employers and employees, the former paying higher prices per piece than required and the latter receiving poor wages.

This system, with its "bickering, quarreling, and . . . hard feeling . . . between the two sides," need not continue.[6] A contrasting high-wage/low-labor-cost system can be created if organizations generate the necessary information. This means developing procedures for completing work more quickly and efficiently. A major component of such development is work time study, deconstructing jobs into elementary components and studying the time it takes workers to perform each of these actions under varying conditions. The time-and-motion researcher with the cooperation of the workers gets a sense of the best way of handling each component by first recording how long it takes a first-class employee to complete the motions and then adding a given percentage of this time to cover unavoidable delays and interruptions, and rest periods. Comparative experiments then reveal which changes in layout, equipment, or the order of physical motions would improve the time taken for the job.

Time study is not an end in itself. It is one tactic to improve shop production, which itself is simply a strategy to reach the goal of industrial cooperation, the assumption being that employers will be less relentless in pursuing low wages if profits are greater.

Time study does not determine a precise and unvarying count of seconds it takes to do each motion. Any set of experiments is tentative, yielding advances that themselves become subject to later improvements. Taylor never claims that time study yields perfect knowledge of how to labor; all he avers in its defense is that it gives "a vastly closer approximation as to time than we ever had before."[7]

Among the most-often-quoted passages from Taylor's books are vignettes illustrating what he accomplished with accurate time studies at Bethlehem Steel. This material shows how his work studies are applied to what are generally viewed as simple, repetitive, unskilled manual jobs.

Taylor opens one narrative by asserting that "the average man would question whether there is much of any science in the work of shoveling." Yet

> for a first-class shoveler there is a given shovel load at which he will do his biggest day's work. What is this shovel load? Will a first-class man do more work per day with a shovel load of 5 pounds, 10 pounds, 15 pounds, 20, 25, 30, or 40 pounds? Now this is a question which can be answered only through carefully made experiments.[8]

By varying shovel loads, Taylor found that shovelers were most productive with 21 pounds on their shovel. As a result he rescinded Bethlehem's practice of having each worker use his own implement and issued each man a shovel that would hold 21 pounds of whatever material he was lifting, a small one for iron ore and a large one for ashes.

A more elaborate illustration involved loading pig iron on railroad cars. Taylor's research assistant timed its constituent tasks, such as picking up the pig iron from the ground, walking with it on a level and an incline, throwing the iron down and walking back empty to get another load.[9] Based on over three months of observations, Taylor concluded that workers were most productive if they were under load and allowed to rest at specified periods of the day. He offered a worker whom he calls "Schmidt" (actually Henry Knolle) a chance to earn $1.85 a day, rather than the regulation $1.15, if he would follow the researcher's work/rest regimen so that "When he tells you to pick up a pig and walk, you pick it up and you walk, and when he tells you to sit down and rest, you sit down. You do that right straight through the day."[10] Schmidt agreed, and following Taylor's methods he learned to handle 47½ tons per day, rather than the 12½ tons that he and other Bethlehem workers routinely loaded. This meant lower labor costs for Bethlehem and higher wages for an unskilled employee.

The Schmidt episode is often used to castigate Taylor because of the way he describes pig iron loading and the mentality of loaders. Because Taylor wants to emphasize the universality of his methods, he goes to great pains to show that the task is so crude that most people would not associate it with science. He calls it "the most elementary form of labor that is known."[11] To clinch the case he uses two offensive animal analogies.

> This work is so crude and elementary in its nature that the writer firmly believes that it would be possible to train an intelligent gorilla so as to become a more efficient pig-iron handler than any man can be.
>
> Now one of the very first requirements for a man who is fit to handle pig iron as a regular occupation is that he shall be so stupid and so phlegmatic that he more nearly resembles . . . the ox than any other type.[12]

While these remarks are inexcusable, they represent a miniscule fraction of Taylor's writings on work and have to be taken in the context of asserting the importance of studying even such routine labor, rather than a simple assertion that Schmidt himself was a gorilla or an ox. They are a deviation from Taylor's own stricture against being patronizing and condescending, but they cannot be used to assert his contempt for labor; in his letters, he uses equally offensive analogies concerning managers (e.g., financiers as hogs).[13]

The point of the narratives is to leave the skeptical reader "convinced that there is a certain science back of the handling of pig iron,"[14] and other menial chores. Taylor could assert that he had never met a single contractor to whom it had even occurred that there was such a thing as a science of labor. Since the books address practitioners, Taylor uses cases to make his points; he embellishes work stories so that they interest an audience of managers and engineers through their particularity as well as their applications. The stylistic problem is to write entertaining narrative while linking each case with the assertion that all work—no matter how repetitive and manual—benefits from study and experimentation. Taylor's awkward, even offensive, handling of the issue should not obscure the purpose of the stories: to show that "there is no class of work which cannot be profitably submitted to time study," whether pig-iron loading, clerical work, or solving problems in mathematics.[15] While the animal analogies can be argued as showing Taylor's distancing himself from labor, the idea behind his narratives is actually to unite skilled and unskilled work by showing that both are capable of study; the thrust of the narratives is to deny the notion that any work is truly unskilled.

Planning

A new approach to studying work leads inexorably to proposing a new organization structure. Developing and maintaining a valid work science or art requires reorganization, particularly creation of a planning department. This is a central record-keeping repository that stores information derived from time and motion studies and serves as a clearing house, sending instructions to and receiving reports from operating personnel. Besides performing all work experiments, the planning department staff analyze all incoming orders for products, for which they perform required design and drafting, and then route those orders from place to place in the plant. The planning department's written archives supplant the foreman's memory as the repository of information on requests and plans for new work, materials in inventory, cost of items manufactured, pay, and discipline.[16] The company regulates and prints the various forms that the new department requires, including shop reports, time cards, instruction sheets on preferred work methodologies, pay sheets, and storeroom records. As in Metcalfe's arsenal system, these are filled out by the workers and directly submitted to the central repository—bypassing the shop foremen.

With so much new information being created, organizations must abandon the military form of command where each worker reports to a single agent. Functional management is needed, with each worker receiving daily orders and help directly from eight different supervisors, each of whom has a different function.

Located in the planning room are those supervisors concerned principally with recordkeeping—the order-of-work, instruction-card, and time-and-cost clerks—and those who discipline workers for lateness or absences. On the shop floor, the "gang boss" prepares work. The "speed boss" supervises the use of tools and setting of machine speeds. The "inspector" is in charge of quality control. The "repair boss" supervises the care and maintenance of the machines.[17]

Some of these supervisors relate to each individual worker for such short periods that they can function for the entire shop. Other supervisors have heavy hands-on contact, and consequently must oversee only a small group where they "should be not only able but willing to pitch in . . . and show the men how to set the work in record time."[18]

The shop management has to change worker-supervisor grouping under the new Taylor system. Each entry-level employee belongs to eight different aggregations which shift according to the particular functional supervisor who guides him at a given moment. Since Taylor advocates competence in specific tasks (e.g., setting up work or repairing machines) as the basis for supervisory appointment, this system emphasizes the role of knowledge or skill as legitimators of supervisor's authority. It also stresses the disparate skills necessary to run an organization; opportunities for promotion should be found for those with record-keeping abilities, for those who can repair tools, and for those with the many other discrete skills. This is in line with the philosophy that each workman should be given as far as possible the highest grade of work for which his individual ability and physique fit him.[19] A reorganized factory offers many opportunities for promotion not found in a foreman-do-all establishment.

Chance for Success

While optimism pervades Taylor's work, he did not perceive either managers or workers rushing to embrace so novel a system— the first use of work experiments and a pervasive repudiation of the rule that each worker have only one boss. To use Taylor's ideas, every hierarchical level would have to experience a change in its vertical relations from "suspicious watchfulness and antagonism and frequently open enmity . . . to that of friendship."[20] Employees, duped so many times in the past, might find it hard to cooperate during the experimentation and training phases. They might well regard as "impertinent interference" attempts to teach them new ways of handling their chores, unless they can be made to see that the experimentally derived standards were advantageous to their own interests.[21] Managers will be even harder to convince because "money must be spent, and in many cases a great deal of money, before the changes are completed which result in lowering cost."[22]

Conversion requires initial sacrifices at all levels, none more daunting than the need for a "complete revolution in the mental attitude and the habits of all those engaged in . . . management, as well as . . . the workmen."[23] Because the system relies on cooperation, it cannot be imposed by force. If the owners want to convert, they must stress to managers "a broad and comprehensive view of the general objects to be attained,"[24] including the eventual economic usefulness of non-producers such as the trainers and record-keeping clerks.

A convinced manager receives the task of explaining the system to the workers, giving them every chance to express their views. During a two- to five-year period, volunteers are requested for work training and development, no attempt being made to coerce those who prefer using their own methods.

> The first few changes which affect the workmen should be made exceedingly slowly, and only one workman at a time should be dealt with at the start. Until this single man has been thoroughly convinced that a great gain has come to him from the new method, no further change should be made. Then one man after another should be tactfully changed over. After passing the point at which from one-fourth to one-third of the men in the employ of the company have been changed . . . practically all of the workmen who are working under the old system become desirous to share in the benefits which they see have been received by those working in the new plan.[25]

Object lessons—rather than talk—convince employees that experimentation not only aids the company by increasing productivity but helps the workers personally by extending new material and psychic rewards, including higher wages, improved communication and, most important, advancement opportunities. The presence of peers who enjoy these satisfactions convinces the recalcitrants of the superiority of the new methods.

At no point does Taylor predicate workers' conversion based on higher wages alone. A chance to earn more money is cited as a necessary—rather than a sufficient—prerequisite. Taylor states flatly that of more importance still is "the development of each man . . . so that he may be able to do, generally speaking, the highest grade of work for which his natural abilities fit him."[26] It is difficult to see how modern textbooks can speak of "pure" or "sole" economic motivation when Taylor insists that despite the importance of wages, the "most important object . . . should be the training and development."[27] His motivational approach is clearly tri-dimensional, centering on higher wages, improved communication, and opportunities for advancement.

Higher Wages

After training, an employee who performs a suggested fair day's task receives from 30 to 100 percent more per day than the company's previous average pay for that task. A differential piece work system ensures high pay for a large output and lower wages for poorer or more careless performance, giving those who learn the new methods "a good liberal increase, which must be permanent."[28]

Improved Communication

With its emphasis on information flow and new methods, shop management required more two-way communication than the traditional foreman-do-all setup with its extremes of driving or coercing workers and leaving them to their own unaided devices. Taylor was well aware that anxiety develops when workers lack knowledge about how their efforts are viewed. At a time when employees received almost no written feedback, he recommends giving each a slip of paper identifying daily progress on tasks.[29] He suggests bulletin boards to keep work units posted on the status of orders. He insists that

> Each man should be encouraged to discuss any trouble which he may have. . . . Men would far rather even be blamed by their bosses . . . than be passed by day after day without a word.[30]

Interaction includes supervisors' listening to the worker's point of view and reacting with respect to the information they receive so that workers "feel that substantial justice is being done them."[31]

In particular, training involves "close, intimate, personal cooperation between the management and the men," where each worker gets "the most friendly help from those who are over him."[32] At a bicycle ball factory where Taylor consulted,

> each girl was made to feel that she was the object of especial care and interest on the part of management and that if anything went wrong with her she could always have a helper.[33]

For the workers, training involves learning new methods and then suggesting improvements. Taylor notes that "the first step is for each man to learn to obey the laws as they exist, and next, if the laws are wrong, to have them reformed in the proper way."[34] In a factory, this means that the employees learn the planning department's latest methods before suggesting improvements. All suggestions are tested by the planning staff, and if they increase productivity they are adopted by the entire crew.

As a consultant, at the Link Belt Company, Taylor used esteem as a motivator by telling workers he would test their suggestions and name useful changes after those who proposed them. He justifies this by saying, "It is quite a thing for a man to have the best method about the works called Jones' method."[35] Why should this matter at all if money is the sole motivator?

In *Principles* Taylor addresses the charge that training diminishes worker autonomy, that employees lose something if they are not left to their own devices unaided. His reply centers on the anomaly of proscribing training for workers while accepting it for surgeons or dentists, when

> the training of the surgeon has been almost identical in type with the teaching and training which is given to the workman. The surgeon, all through his early years, is under the closest supervision of more experienced men, who show him the minutest way how each element of his work is best done. They provide him with the finest implements, each one of which has been the subject of special study and development, and then insist upon his using each . . . in the very best way.[36]

Only when the student learns the basis of his craft is he invited to "use his originality and ingenuity to make *real additions to the world's knowledge instead of reinventing things which are old.*"[37] The only innovation in worker training is in extending education to the factory, providing the shoveler with an activity normally reserved for his "betters" with high school and college diplomas. A painful discrepancy exists when people praise academic education for a small elite and disparage efforts to teach manual workers better ways to handle their jobs, reinforcing a distinction between work that requires skill and work that needs no particular ability. Taylor sees no such distinction, noting that,

> if it were true that the workman would develop into a larger and finer man without all this teaching . . . then it would follow that the young man who now comes to college to have the help of a teacher in mathematics, physics, chemistry, Latin, Greek, etc., would do better to study these things unaided and by himself.[38]

Yet no one suggests solitary academic labor as a generic alternative to universities. At the academic level, the advantages of teacher-pupil interaction are clear. Why is the person at the bottom of the hierarchy the only one who cannot benefit from education?

A letter from an Australian judge extends this analogy to the arts, a field Taylor relied on as much as the sciences for a model of how careful preparation is prerequisite to real discovery. Taylor was fond of quoting Judge Charles Heydon's assertion that music teachers were longstanding shop management advocates because they knew that the "genius who plays the piano without having been taught the proper, i.e., the most efficient method of fingering, will come short of his very best."[39] Why should imposed technique serve the artist and stifle the pig-iron loader? Why should specialized training not serve as a foundation for helping each do a proper task?

Modern management theory emphasizes the importance of training and feedback.[40] A recent article uses the artistic analogy for a strongly argued proposition that freedom in organizations cannot occur without training. In words that would have engaged Taylor, political scientist Larry Preston notes that creativity is only

> possible for those who have mastered established ideas and practices. . . . The virtuoso pianist, exemplifying creative freedom at the keyboard, builds on years of training and practice. And his or her creativity is primarily an extension of the methods developed and learned by past teachers and masters of the piano. No one sits at a piano and invents a technique. . . . If we want to enhance individuals' freedom, we must be willing to provide an understanding of prevailing practices and the resources needed to decide and act with respect to them.[41]

Taylor does not expect the full-time line worker to have as many new ideas as people performing experiments all day, since the full-time worker lacks the time for and habits of generalizing— which seems obvious and does not raise hackles with regard to professions. Do general practitioners discover as many new drugs as researchers attached to universities? Is it elitist to name this disparity?[42] He does insist that workers who suggest improvements be given encouragement and full credit when their innovations are useful. Through such procedures, "the true initiative of the workman is better attained under scientific management than under the old individual plan."[43]

Training and concomitant two-way communication are important motivators both directly and in permitting the company to offer a career ladder where each person is challenged by the highest grade of work that he can learn to perform well. Education not only facilitates workers' mastering their own jobs but it enables the company to groom the most able for higher-paying tasks or lateral transfers where people who are poor at one job may prove excellent at another.[44] Training accompanied by structural reorganization sets the stage for those advancement opportunities that Taylor sees as the ultimate motivational strategy.

Opportunities for Advancement

Creating a career ladder is a paramount "duty of employers . . . both in their own interest and in that of their employees."[45] Both *Shop Management* and *Principles* assert the motivational power of having

> the laborer who before was unable to do anything beyond, perhaps shoveling and wheeling dirt from place to place . . . taught to do the more elementary machinist's work, accompanied by the agreeable surroundings and the interesting variety and higher wages which go with the machinist's trade,[46]

while at the same time, the best "machinists become functional foremen and teachers. And so on, right up the line."[47]

Training enables workers to learn more highly skilled work that might well have been closed to them in the past. Functional restructuring demands

> a larger number of men in this class, so that men, who must otherwise have remained machinists all their lives, will have the opportunity of rising to a foremanship.[48]

New opportunities to do "much higher, more interesting, and finally more developing" work are an important motivational strategy.[49]

Some of Taylor's modern critics condemn functional foremanship for creating "a master class of scientific managers ruling over a servant class of workers."[50] This anachronistic criticism is predicated on modern corporate personnel practices, where few, if any, managerial vacancies are filled by blue-collar workers without college degrees. Taylor makes it perfectly clear that he intends to use the most competent workers to fill executive positions without regard to academic credentialing because the most vital managerial attributes are "grit" and "constructive imagination" and "success at college or the technical school does not indicate the presence of these qualities, even though the man may have worked hard."[51] In a letter to Edwin Gay, dean of Harvard University's Graduate Business School, he objects to graduates appearing at factories to inquire if they can commence their careers with shop-management research; he notes that "one trouble with the man who has had a very extensive academic education is that he fails to see any good coming to him from long continued work as a workman," while Taylor, on the contrary, sees such long, continued work as the best way to learn how to plan and manage work experiments.[52] Managers and workers do not constitute autonomous classes; task labor is the advocated route into task management.[53] *Principles* contains an oblique warning against managers trying to install scientific management without taking the time and trouble to train employees as functional foremen and teachers so that their very presence serves as an object lesson on the new system's personal benefits.[54] Possibilities for promotion are an essential feature of a system that emphasizes cooperation, one whose technical mechanism of time study should not be

> used more or less as a club to drive the workmen, against their wishes . . . to work much harder, instead of gradually teaching and leading them towards new methods, and convincing them through object-lessons that task management means for them somewhat harder work, but also far greater prosperity.[55]

Chapter 5

Immediate Reception

Taylor wrote to precipitate action—immediate, measurable results. He told an associate, "the people whom I want to reach . . . are principally those men who are doing the manufacturing and construction work of our country, both employers and employees."[1] To interest such a large, variegated audience, he insisted on giving his books a narrative form, including recital of anecdotes with semifictional dialogue. He changed the title of his second book from *Philosophy of Scientific Management* to *Principles*, noting, "I am afraid that the word 'philosophy' in the title will tend to make the thing sound rather high-falutin."[2]

The man's language often seems coarse to the modern scholar's ear, particularly the language in the Schmidt anecdotes. While one cause of this may lie in the passage of time (we think we are more honest in our expression than our grandparents, but we have our own circumlocutions), Taylor's insistence on using unvarnished shop-floor language elicited complaints from his own associates. One, Morris Cooke, notes,

> The term "Gang Boss" especially seems to me objectionable and out of harmony with the spirit of scientific management. . . . The word "supervisor" seems to me to be better adapted to our business.[3]

Here, Taylor is cautioned to use a softer word with positive personnel-management connotations, a request he quickly denies, noting, "I . . . do not like 'supervisor.' "[4] "Gang boss" it remained, Taylor's delight in actual shop-floor expressions overwhelming any interest in using more academically respectable nomenclature.

Just as Taylor decried the gulf between skilled and unskilled work, he also tried to break down the conceptual distinction between professional and popular publishing. He takes the stance that his work can have professional insights worthy of discussion at ASME meetings while at the same time being couched in popular prose for publication in *American Magazine* with its mass circulation. Again Cooke remonstrates:

> The principal disadvantage of publishing in this magazine is that you are a technical man and that until quite recently it was not considered good professional practice for technical men to use mediums of this kind for bringing out new scientific doctrine.[5]

Taylor ignored this criticism, his goal being to provide technical information to a mass audience, not a summary of technical data (say, a three-page article based on *Principles*), but the identical message presented to people who shared his educational pedigree. At his own expense, he printed copies of *Principles* for all ASME members while seeing to its *American Magazine* serialization.[6] This ensured simultaneous scholarly and popular discussion.

The decade before America entered World War I saw extensive professional and popular-press debate over Taylor's theories. A 1912 ASME committee described the work as spawning enthusiastic advocates and vigorous opponents.[7] As Taylor foresaw, his ideas also produced a sizable cadre of managers who borrowed discrete techniques (e.g., time study and differential piece rates) while abjuring the underlying principles of cooperation, employee development, and mutual gain. Although Taylor vigorously criticized those who borrowed discrete aspects of his system, many outsiders confused their practice with Taylor's theories. The written legacy produced by adherents, opponents, and those who used only some aspects of Taylorism gives a unique picture of scientific management as it was viewed in its own time. The work of Taylor's supporters is particularly interesting because it stresses facets totally absent from most modern textbooks.

Adherents

From the Midvale years on, Taylor was the center of a small circle of engineer acolytes. Henry Gantt and Carl Barth (his Midvale assistants) were charter members. Others include Horace Hathaway, hired to help Barth improve the Link Belt Company's productivity in 1904, and Morris Cooke, a publishing executive.

Outside this group, scientific management was most attractive to public-sector-oriented Progressive reformers rather than to business leaders.[8] The first quarter of the twentieth century marks the heyday of Progressivism, a pervasive but diffuse political movement based on the belief that (1) a corrupt political system benefited a few rich people at the poor's expense and (2) planned progress towards a better system was possible as well as desirable. Typical Progressives condemned some excesses of the new plutocracy and were in full cry against monopoly, but they were not anti-business. They accepted the large corporate industrial capitalist system as a natural product of social evolution, and associated its evils with particular corrupt financiers and acts of fraud. They were fundamentally conservative to the extent that they offered programs that did not alter business supremacy over the control of wealth, although they sympathized with the workers whom they viewed as underdogs. They displayed a Taylorite optimism in believing that a good society would, should, and could alleviate the lot of poor people.[9]

In the legal sphere, the movement pressed for specific governmental changes to push the country towards reform, some affecting procedures (for example, direct primaries, initiatives, referenda) and others, policy (child labor laws, progressive income taxes, etc.). On the local level, sympathizers opposed electoral "machines," which were generally viewed as corrupt.

Key Progressives perceived shop management as a means for initiating organizational reform on a manageable and practical scale without damaging business. Taylor's views on training were congenial to professionals (lawyers, ministers, college professors) who loomed large in the reform ranks and whose own status depended on training that enabled them to apply a corpus of knowledge and techniques on the job. Taylor's ideas seemed to offer an equivalent way of increasing the satisfaction and esteem of blue-collar factory occupations. The notion that scientific management decreased the conceptual gap between the status-rich professions and the underdog workers led one adherent to label the theory "part of a larger movement, the realization of a sense of social solidarity, of social responsibility of each for all."[10]

The muckraker, Ida Tarbell, stresses this interpretation in a series of *American Magazine* articles asserting that scientific management dignifies factory labor by considering it worthy of study, thus eliminating any skilled–unskilled dichotomy.[11] Tarbell also paints a very positive picture of the human-relations changes wrought by the new management style. Her narrative places Taylor as a New England Butt Company consultant holding open meetings to explain the project's benefits for the workers, describing the information he needs to collect and its usefulness, giving his audience a chance to ask questions and raise objections to participating in work experiments. The new system is described in terms of its psychological advantages to the worker's self-respect and its propensity to minimize arbitrary orders that can now be challenged on the basis of data learned in training or by calling for experimentation. Tarbell echoes Taylor himself in considering higher wages only one motivation for participation in the new mode of worker-manager relations; the opportunity for training and a chance to rise through the ranks and perform more varied and interesting tasks are also motivating.

One suprise Tarbell has for the modern reader is her assumption that scientific management's principal opponents will be selfish employers who resist diminution of arbitrary power, who prefer the role of taskmasters to experimenters and educators. Her title, "The Golden Rule in Business," indicates her missionary zeal to convert old-fashioned employers and her understanding that scientific management enables executives to treat a laborer as they themselves would wish to be treated. Her work emphasizes the centripetal aspect of Taylor's ideas, how their implementation bridges the gap between the treatment of skilled and unskilled employees.

Taylor demonstrated his relation to Tarbell and other Progressives by serializing *Principles* in *American Magazine,* a journal known for publishing reform writers. Its editor solicited the manuscript because of his interest in "insurgency," acknowledging that Taylor and his associates represented the insurgents in the factory management sphere.[12]

Cautioned against publishing in a radical journal, Taylor answers in language that gives the lie to his personally favoring factory owners over employees:

> Among a certain class of people the *American Magazine* is looked upon as a muck-raking magazine. I think that any magazine which opposed the "stand-patters" and was not under the control of the moneyed powers of the United States would now be classed among the muck-rakers. This, therefore, has no very great weight with me.[13]

Before World War I, ASME conferences often erupted into imbroglios between Progressives and "stand-patters." The reformist

faction found a staunch ally in Taylor, whose stance in these controversies almost always weighed in against the short-term economic
interests of factory owners. He unsuccessfully fought to have the
society sponsor a section on public matters that would investigate
how industrial practices such as polluting affected city life. In April
1909, he signed a petition requesting that the Association hold a
conference on air pollution, open to the public and including speak-
ers from the public health field, a request that the society's officers,
under pressure from industry, denied.[14] His official biographer
quotes him as saying shortly before his death, "Throughout my life
I have been very much inclined toward the radical side in all
things."[15] This is almost certainly an avowal of Progressive leaning.

Brandeis

Taylor's most useful Progressive adherent was Louis Dembitz
Brandeis, known in his day as "the people's lawyer."[16] Brandeis
originally approached Taylor for help in a difficult case. In the
spring of 1910, the railroads east of the Mississippi gave their employees a pay raise and applied to the Interstate Commerce Commission (ICC) for permission to raise freight rates. Brandeis saw this
move as a corporate attempt to recoup operating losses by over-
charging consumers. Representing the Trade Association of the At-
lantic Seaboard as unpaid counsel, he opposed the increase,
arguing that the railroads could support the pay hike through more
efficient management.[17]

Hearings in Washington, D.C. began on October 12, 1910. Two
weeks later, Brandeis wrote Taylor, asking for data on scientific
management (a term he seems to have coined—Taylor previously
used "shop management" or "task management"). Readers of post-
World-War-II textbooks might surmise that Taylor would reply by
explaining how his system motivates worker productivity through
higher wages. But those who have read Taylor's own books will be
ready for his return letter outlining the system's use of noneconomic motivation. Taylor asserts that shop management democra-
tizes the plant and removes class distinctions by extending training
to all. The system provides new advancement opportunities, increasing worker ambition.[18]

Taylor asked Morris Cooke and Henry Gantt to work with
Brandeis on his presentation. Gantt was particularly active. He unsuccessfully tried to persuade the ASME council to endorse the
anti-increase brief.[19] He testified at the hearing, reiterating Taylor's

emphasis on noneconomic motivation, gains the system brings by checking arbitrary supervisors and allowing talented mechanics to rise into the planning department. Scientific management increases worker performance because,

> we get from our men . . . who have worked at routine work . . . the material for more responsible positions. . . . Inefficiency in the workman is not his fault. . . . We have spent a tremendous amount of money in developing machinery and . . . very little money in developing men.[20]

The hearings proved a publicity bonanza. A February 1911 ICC decision against the railroads was one factor that propelled scientific management into people's minds. Taylor thanked Brandeis for bringing his theories to wide public notice.[21]

Had Brandeis simply appropriated scientific management to win a case, he would have relinquished his interest after the victory. In reality, he made it a point to advocate Taylor's approach in a wide array of later speeches. At the 1912 Brown University commencement, he stresses the Taylor system's cooperative basis, noting, "The old idea of a good bargain was a transaction in which one man got the better of another. The new idea . . . is a transaction which is good for both parties to it."[22] At a talk before the Boston Central Labor Union Brandeis stressed how training gives employers a stake in conserving labor. Even unscrupulous owners will not want to arbitrarily fire or overwork people in whom they have invested development money.[23]

Brandeis' forward to Frank Gilbreth's *Primer of Scientific Management* emphasizes the system's equalizing effect through training and promotion opportunities that afford workers a chance for the same self-respect and satisfaction held by professionals.[24] A 1920 address in the Taylor Society's memorial volume notes that scientific management "makes the hire worthy of the laborer," and with Progressive optimism proposes that its impact may be to "make work . . . the greatest of life's joys.[25] Brandeis' understanding of scientific management is very close to Tarbell's. Both had an interest in Taylor's ideas because they believed his system would bring workers material and nonmaterial benefits and bridge the gap between professionals and factory labor. The Taylorism they support foreshadows much of Elton Mayo's advocacy of better human relations in the factory and the work-as-motivator insights currently credited to Douglas McGregor and Abraham Maslow. While neither Brandeis

nor Tarbell can be considered radicals in the sense that either
wanted to replace the economic dominance of the corporate sector,
they were concerned with meliorist changes from noneconomic motivation, particularly the increase in worker self-respect and interest
that develops from training and a chance at frequent promotion.

Opponents

Taylor's earliest opponents were old-line plant managers ob-
jecting to the fiscal implications of higher wages and company-
sponsored training[26] and foremen jealous of their traditional
prerogatives. Few modern summaries of Taylor analyze this rebuttal
of Taylor's work, but *Shop Management* labels "the opposition of the
heads of departments and the foremen and the gang bosses . . . the
greatest problem in organization."[27] Taylor asserts that he can more
readily persuade workers to try the new way than superintendents
and foremen.

A second, somewhat later antagonist was the American Feder-
ation of Labor (AFL). Representing skilled workers, it argued that
scientific management was a ploy to break their members' monopo-
lies on shop expertise.[28] For union leaders, the time-study man was
sent into the factory to steal their members' trade secrets, thus enabling employers to fire them and hire unskilled laborers at low
wages and train them to perform those craft tasks, heretofore the
province of the small elite possessing the requisite skills. Frank
Hudson sums up the union view in a thoughtful *American Machinist*
article in 1911 expressing a willingness to hear about better methods
but rejecting company-wide training.[29] An International Association
of Machinists circular of April 1911 denounces the system for enabling companies to hire unskilled manual laborers for machinist
positions, which "will mean the wiping out of our trade and organization with the accompanying low wages, life-destroying hard
work, long hours and intolerable conditions generally."[30]

Labor opposition may have surprised Taylor more than managerial intransigence because he was not intrinsically anti-union,
while his work does attack prevailing managerial practices. He saw
a necessary union role in traditional factories without other channels for curbing authority. To a Harvard business school professor,
he wrote that he is "heartily in favor of unions" where the employer
is a hog or careless of employee rights.[31] *Shop Management* states:

> When employers herd their men together in classes, pay all of
> each class the same wages, and offer none of them any induce-

ments to work harder or do better than the average, the only remedy for the men lies in combination; and frequently the only possible answer to encroachments on the part of their employers is a strike.[32]

However, he did believe that scientific management would supplant the trade union movement as a means of helping the worker, that as scientific management increased productivity, employers would be able to raise wages and shorten work weeks, thus eliminating the need to bargain over these issues. With workers and managers cooperating to develop better methods together, "the close, intimate cooperation, the constant personal contact . . . will tend to diminish friction and discontent," thus eliminating almost all causes for dispute and disagreement.[33]

He agreed with Brandeis—generally considered a union sympathizer—who writes, "There is absolutely nothing in scientific business management opposed to organized labor."[34] He believed that workers and right-thinking managers could cooperate in a manager-initiated system, a view that may have appeared naive to union leaders, who would have asked, "Where is the evidence?"

Modern works dealing with Taylor make few if any references to his old-line manager opposition, with its reactionary complaints that now seem so irrelevant. Much more is written about the AFL critique, spearheaded by the International Association of Machinists, which does seem to bolster scientific management's anti-labor image. It is easy to read the quarrel as Exeter-educated "have" versus blue-collar "have nots." This obscures the fact that union opposition represented labor's own elite fighting to prevent less fortunate or less skilled workers from taking even a few steps up the factory ladder.

Taylor argues that his system benefits all workers:

It is true, for instance, that the planning room, and functional foremanship, render it possible for an intelligent laborer or helper in time to do much of the work now done by a machinist. Is not this a good thing for the laborer and helper? He is given a higher class of work, which tends to develop him and gives him better wages.

[Concurrently,] the machinist, with the aid of the new system, will rise to a higher class of work which he was unable to do in the past, and in addition, divided or functional foremanship will call for a larger number of men in this class, so that men, who must otherwise have remained machinists all their lives, will have the opportunity of rising to a foremanship.[35]

The International Association of Machinists protested the lumping together of their members who do not become foremen with people who start as common laborers, thus diluting the pool of skilled workers and making it easier to hire machinists at low wages. The association's quarrel with Taylor is partly a matter of vantage point. Quite understandably, the union is concerned with the welfare of its members. While Taylor can assert, "In the sympathy for the machinist the case of the laborer is overlooked,"[36] the association is in business to ignore the laborers when their interests conflict with the AFL machinists. (The quarrel might have been totally different if helper/laborer unions had existed in 1911.)

To some extent the controversy can be clarified with empirical evidence. What happens when a factory adopts some scientific management variant? Do machinist wages sink? Are unskilled laborers eventually promoted?

Some empirical support does exist supporting the contention that scientific management in practice brings machinists closer to the status of laborers; but it does so by raising the unskilled workers rather than tangibly lowering the machinists. In 1915, Robert Hoxie, by no means a Taylor supporter, studied factories that had adopted some variant of scientific management. He concludes that the new system tends to realign wages, leveling the skilled/unskilled disparity but that it does so by raising the pay of the unskilled.[37] What the craft workers are protesting is a decline in relative financial superiority. This is an understandable cause for a proud machinists' union but hardly an appropriate one for a battle of "haves" and "have nots."

The second union fear is that planning departments cut the worker's independence and use of his own good judgment.[38] To the extent that planning departments standardize tools and methodologies, this cutback is inherent in the system. The defense is that the best workers move into the planning department, which encourages suggestions from employees working on the shop floor.

Particularly after 1911, Taylor tried to respond to union criticisms. He arranged for the president of the Boot and Shoe Makers Union to talk to workers at plants where he had consulted. Morris Cooke writes

I think the most important thing to be accomplished by his visit is to convince him beyond any doubt that we really mean it when we say that our relations with the workmen are not only friendly but are of such a nature that it will be impossible for him to find any of them who will criticize what we are doing.[39]

In addition, Taylor fought to break the easy assumption that any company using time and motion studies was actually committed to his ideas. No union chief was ever angrier than Taylor himself at managers adopting his mechanisms as a club to force workers into higher productivity. He realized quite early that his worst enemies were managers who borrowed some of his mechanical devices (notably the stopwatch) without any commitment to his aim at cooperation and increased benefits for all. Specific union complaints were often based on misapplications of his system—even when such misapplications contradicted explicit arguments in his major works.

To the extent that Taylor perceived managers as his worst enemies, he loses points as a prophet. The union critique has been much more damaging, particularly in the political arena. The only salve for his prophetic ego could be his contention that the union critique stemmed from managerial misapplication of his methods, that the AFL distrust arose from managerial antagonism to change in basic reward patterns. Complaints about a planning room divorced from workers cannot stem from *Shop Management* or *Principles*, both of which make abundantly clear that the workers rise to the planning department. Such complaints can come as a reaction to managers bent on using time study and centralization to extract gain for management alone. With this interpretation, the way to minimize union dissent is to eliminate managerial misapplication. In practical terms, this means condemning half-hearted imitators borrowing specific mechanisms but not the new system's underlying philosophy, those who time employees' work but will not create a planning department staffed by the workers.

Imitators

As early as his time at Bethlehem, Taylor was forced to realize that the committed enthusiast and the workaday line manager have radically different perspectives. The theorist can afford to emphasize the long-term benefits of two-way communication and worker training. Most managers are more concerned with short-term profits even if they consider human relations worthwhile.

Taylor's system contains practices that may increase short-term productivity without helping the workers. A company can force its workers to have their motions timed and then enforce new production quotas based on the knowledge obtained. This violates Taylor's explicit stricture against timing without consent, and certainly cannot be considered an aspect of the Taylor system. But why should managers focused on the present bother with consent, when, as Henry Gantt notes, "people value these methods only as new ways of controlling workmen . . . a chance to get something for nothing."[40]

A new occupation soon arose made up of engineering consultants offering to systematize plants by using some of Taylor's methods but with shortcuts, such as testing work time without prior explanations or worker permission. In January 1910, for example, Taylor complained to Cooke that commentators were associating their names with consulting work done at the American Locomotive Company:

> In reality, the facts are that our methods were not all being used there. Harrington Emerson went there with his various shortcuts . . . and Van Alstyne had a whole lot more shortcuts of his own, and then enforced all of this with a club. Now this combination, which uses many of the details of our system and leaves out the essential underlying principles, is the worst thing that can happen to us. Van Alystne has used time study as a club, not as a means of harmonizing the interests of employers and employees.[41]

To separate his ideas from those of such imitators, Taylor refused to join the National Society for Promoting Efficiency nor the New York and Philadelphia Efficiency Societies because Harrington Emerson and other perceived half-way implementers were members.[42] Explaining his conduct, he notes

> All the world, of course, wants Efficiency now, as it has always wanted it. This is not, however, a sufficient basis for a group of men to get together any more than you would get together a society of men, say, to be good. All the world wants to be good.
> It is only when you have some particular scheme for promoting goodness that people are able to get together profitably.[43]

Taylor was intent on distinguishing his "scheme" from that of other engineer consultants.

The most destructive conflation of Taylor and his imitators occurs in recrimination over the Watertown arsenal strike. Because management tactics leading to the strike misused scientific management—and were explicitly objected to by Taylor before the labor unrest—it is important to examine and disentangle this particular conflation.

Watertown Arsenal

In January 1909, General William Crozier, head of the Army Ordnance Department, visited Taylor in Germantown, Pennsylvania, to learn how standardizing tools might improve arsenal production.[44] During the next half year, Taylor met personally and corresponded with Crozier about using scientific management in armament manufacture, eventually recommending that Carl Barth reorganize the machine shop at Watertown Arsenal in Massachusetts.

Controversy hung over Crozier's efforts. At its Washington headquarters, the International Association of Machinists issued an anti-Taylor circular urging workers to complain to their congressman.[45] In the plant itself, many workers were afraid that any pay gains Barth brought would be temporary because of subsequent rate cuts, an understandable fear with such cuts common at the turn of the century.[46]

Some of the foremen objected to using incentives to reward workers instead of simply punishing the less productive. One supervisor proclaimed:

> If a man is so lazy—to use no better word—that he will not do a day's work without being put on a premium system, he should be immediately removed from the shop and a better man put in his place.[47]

Barth arrived at the arsenal in June 1909, and did little to dispel the controversy, by, for example, soliciting input from the machinist's union. He did follow Taylor's injunction to involve the workers from the start and show them how the new system benefits them in both material and noneconomic ways. An early step was creating a planning department staffed from men in the machine shop. The arsenal's master mechanic was put in charge, with three long-time foremen serving as assistants. Gang boss promotions went to three workers who now had the responsibility to route information between the planning room and the shop floor.[48]

Dwight Merrick, the time-study person, did not arrive until May 1911, when the machine-shop workers could already see that Barth's presence had brought promotions to some of their own. Following Taylor's advice, Merrick explained why he was bringing a stop watch into the plant. No worker was timed without that person's consent. When one machinist complained that the watch made him nervous, Merrick stopped timing his motions.[49] At least one foreman recalled challenging planning-room methods and having these methods changed after proper experimentation.[50]

This process of consultation and consent looked incredibly drawn out to some of the officers for whom it was an idealistic and unworkable method to increase production. Major Clarence Williams showed his displeasure by telling a machinist who was complaining about a planning department method, "Shut right up."[51]

By June 1911, Barth was encountering pressure from Arsenal officers to either speed up his work or allow them to implement an incentive plan of their own choosing in the foundry. Taylor immediately warned Crozier that such action would bring labor trouble; the necessary change was not a speedier system but more understanding by the officers of the workers' fears through more contact between them.[52] Taylor's advice is clear:

> If you go right straight ahead in introducing our system, one step after another, and do not attempt short cuts and do not try to hurry it too fast . . . you will meet with practically no opposition.[53]

Taylor might have been able to withstand the officers' pressure. But in August 1911, Barth gave in to the complaints of Lieutenant Colonel Charles Wheeler and Major Williams, permitting them to introduce their own incentive plan in the foundry, as long as they understood that their process did not represent an application of Taylor's methods.[54]

On August 10, with Barth absent from the arsenal, Wheeler and Williams introduced time study into the foundry without any prior preparation. No planning department had been created to show that changes might develop and promote workers. No explanations were offered for the presence in the foundry of Merrick and his stop watch; certainly the officers wasted no time soliciting permission for timing their own subordinates' motions. Shifting Merrick to the foundry was, in itself, a violation of Taylor's dictum that a time-study person has to know the task.[55] Merrick had a background in machine shop work and knew very little about foundry molding, a point that became painfully apparent as he tried to time specific motions.

After the first day's timing, the molders met informally and agreed not to cooperate with any of Merrick's attempts to time their labor, and to compose a petition protesting the new shop techniques. The next morning, an unsuspecting Merrick arrived at the foundry brandishing his stop watch. He first tried to time Joseph Cooney who, adhering to the molder's decision, refused to work with Merrick standing nearby. After a heated exchange, Merrick called Major Williams, who ordered Cooney to cooperate (a clear violation of Taylor's written advice and quite the contrary of Barth's practice in the machine shop). Cooney again refused. To Williams this was gross insubordination. He discharged Cooney, sparking a mass exit from the foundry.

The strike lasted until August 18, when Colonel Wheeler promised Cooney's reinstatement and an Ordnance Department investigation of the new management techniques. For the molders, the job action was brief and inconclusive, for the changes continued while the investigation was in progress. The major consequence of Cooney's dismissal lay in its publicity value for the International Association of Machinists' campaign against Taylorism. Although the job action did not encompass the association's members, it forged an emotional focus for calls to end the timing of work motions. Because the arsenals were public organizations, with public funding, the union lobbied Congress to examine the Taylor system and prohibit further government agency use of stop watches and premium pay. Under the chairmanship of William Wilson (Dem., Pa.), a former United Mine Workers' official, the House Labor Committee heard a request for such examination from James O'Connell, International Association of Machinists' president, and Nick Alifas, a local Machinists' official, but none, interestingly, from any molders or other workers employed at Watertown.[56] On August 21, the Committee appointed a three-person group to investigate the Taylor system—the first of many attempts to link the foundry strike and Taylor's theories, rather than to see the job action as a result of repudiating Taylor's principles.

Those closest to the situation appreciated the difference. Taylor himself saw the strike as validating his concern with worker involvement. To Cooke he wrote, "This ought to be a warning not to try to hurry task work too fast."[57] Crozier receives a harsher message:

No time study whatever should have been undertaken in the foundry. You will remember that I have told you time and again that without a whole lot of preliminary training no set of workmen should be subjected to the ordeal of time study.[58]

Barth laments that "in the eyes of the world, the Taylor system is responsible for the trouble, while the fact is that the real Taylor system man at the Arsenal has never . . . been inside the foundry."[59] More strikingly, the molder's own lawyer noted "the system in operation is not either the Taylor system or scientific management according to the principles of Frederick W. Taylor."[60] An exhaustive modern study of the strike concludes, "Wheeler and Williams were clear in their own minds that they were not installing the Taylor system."[61] If public administration textbooks want to write about the "Wheeler/Williams management theory," they can use Watertown as an example of these officers' gross insensitivities; the only thing the strike tells us about Taylor's ideas is that they are relatively easy to misapply, a point which does constitute a deficiency in an imperfect world but hardly the deficiency for which he is usually held culpable. Taylor was correct in perceiving that people like Wheeler and Williams were more dangerous to him than committed opponents. No old-line manager, no union chief acting alone could have caused the intense public scrutiny following the foundry strike. Only two partial imitators could have precipitated the House hearings. Antagonism mounted after misapplied attempts to study work without worker involvement in the use of that knowledge to create incentive schemes.

Congressional Hearings: Attack and Rebuttal

The House hearings, which lasted from October 1911 to February 1912, took place before a committee chaired by Representative William Wilson and consisting in addition of William Redfield (Dem., N.Y.) and John Tilson (Rep., Conn.). The committee's composition provided an aura of impartiality, given Wilson's labor background and Redfield's pre-politics business career, an impartiality furnished a further *post hoc* seal of approval when President Woodrow Wilson appointed Redfield Secretary of Commerce and William Wilson Secretary of Labor in 1914.

Taylor's opponents hoped that the hearing would lead to a condemnation of his ideas as oppressive.[62] But by organizing a public forum, they gave their target an unprecedented opportunity to clarify his ideas and distinguish them from imitations. Brandeis, fully aware of the session's publicity value, warned his friend that it was crucial to let the legislature "see scientific management as it is, and not as it is represented."[63]

Taylor, who enjoyed verbal combat, gave twelve hours of testimony spread over four days in January 1912. He challenged the testimony of people who spoke against his system without having read any of his books.[64] His evidence has particular importance because it explicitly rebuts the picture that dominates modern public administration, a portrait that actually seems to describe what he considered misapplications rather than his original theory.

Post-World-War-II public administration literature often argues that Taylorism enthrones efficiency as a public goal.[65] But the January 25, 1912, testimony states: "Scientific management is not any efficiency device, not a device of any kind for securing efficiency; nor is it any bunch or group of efficiency devices."[66] Its goal is a mental change in managers and workers with "the substitution of hearty brotherly cooperation for contention and strife; of both pulling hard in the same direction instead of pulling apart."[67] Efficiency is only important as a means enabling managers and workers to

> take their eyes off of the division of the surplus as the all-important matter, and together turn their attention toward increasing the size of the surplus until this surplus becomes so large that it is unnecessary to quarrel over how it shall be divided.[68]

Since elements associated with increased efficiency (e.g., time studies) can be used "for good and for bad," the intention to cooperate is the only way of differentiating adherents of scientific management.[69] An employer may well increase production by wielding a club, but he is not thus advancing the goals of Taylorism, for "without this complete mental revolution of both sides, scientific management does not exist."[70]

The testimony reiterates Taylor's insistence that time and motion studies require worker agreement, with volunteers recruited through a variety of economic and ego rewards. He suggests the following for recruiting shovelers, for example:

> See here, Pat and Mike, you fellows understand your job all right; both of you fellows are first-class men; you know what we think of you; you are all right now; but we want to pay you

fellows doubles wages. We are going to ask you to do a lot of damn fool things, and when you are doing them there is going to be some one out alongside of you all the time, a young chap with a piece of paper and a stop watch and pencil. . . . Now we want to know whether you fellows want to go into that bargain or not? If you want double wages while that is going on all right, we will pay you double; if you don't, all right, you needn't take the job unless you want to; we just called you in to see if you want to work this way or not.[71]

While this sounds patronizing to the modern ear, it is a long way from Major William's insistence on firing workers who would not cooperate; one method should not be confused with the other.

Taylor also reiterates his insistance on urging workers to challenge the planning department's methods. Before any change occurs, a manager should say:

Try the methods and implements which we give you . . . and then after you have tried our way if you think of an implement or method better than ours, for God's sake come and tell us about it and then we will make an experiment to prove whether your method or ours is the best, and you, as a workman, will be allowed to participate in that experiment.[72]

This give and take is not window dressing but, for Taylor, absolutely crucial as a way of making progress.[73] (General Crozier noted that challenges were allowed by Barth in the Watertown machine shop, where each worker had "the privilege of raising any point he desires and of having it attended to."[74])

The testimony also records Taylor's emphasis on worker development. One motivation is that "in most cases those who set the daily tasks have come quite recently from doing work at their trades."[75] Union fears about scientific management's eliminating skilled jobs are goundless because what actually should happen is that the best workers are transferred to the management domain as "teachers, guiders, and helpers."[76] This means higher wages and more interesting work, two sources of worker satisfaction. Fewer hands needed at machines is good for workers as long as factories are restructured to need more supervisors and planning personnel.

Concurrent with Taylor's testimony, the ASME subcommittee on administration prepared a report reiterating several of the key points in the House exposition. This nine-member committee, chaired by Progressive businessman James Dodge, stressed the new management system's "appreciation of the human factor" with its potential for educating workers and gaining their cooperation.[77] Taylor, present at the group's discussions, agreed that good relations were essential, a point that Wheeler and Williams seem to have proved beyond possibility of refutation.

The work of the ASME group may have played a role in the House committee's final determination on scientific management. Taylor's own testimony certainly influenced the conclusion that no evidence existed to label his system injurious to workers. The machinists union had lobbied for the hearing to produce a report attacking the new system. The actual outcome was inconclusive; it did not provide the union with the desired victory. The army continued to use its version of the new methods in arsenals; in direct outcome, the hearings protected Taylor as well as his imitators.

Dietrick Amendment

Despite this setback, the machinists union continued to lobby legislators to end time-and-motion studies in arsenals. One politician who pledged his support was Representative Frederick Dietrick, from the Watertown arsenal district, who succeeded in putting a rider on the 1914 Army and Navy Appropriations Bills to supress such research and payment premiums in government-managed armaments manufacture.

Dietrick made no pretense at being an expert on Taylor's ideas. According to his own testimony, he had not read the two major books in their entirety, and what he had perused he had not always been able to understand[78] (an amazing admission since the volumes were written for the average high school graduate). His amendments to the appropriations bills were, obviously, not directed against scientific management as theory but rather its practical application at the Watertown Arsenal and, to an even greater extent perhaps, its reputation with the International Association of Machinists as a way to eliminate their crafts.

The riders passed the House but not the Senate. This meant that two versions of both bills were sent to the joint Congressional Legislative Conference Committee for reconciliation. By chance, the committee chose to handle the Navy bill first. Since the Navy was not engaged in time-and-motion studies, its officers made no objection to using the House language against such research, and when the Army bill was handled afterwards this precedent was allowed

to stand. A recent case study of this reconciliation process concludes, "If the Army Bill had been taken up first, the result might
have been different."[79] But the Dietrick amendments did pass. The
International Association of Machinists achieved a notable political
victory—stop watches and premium pay were henceforth banned
from federal armed forces production operations.

The American poet John Greenleaf Whittier notes:

Of all sad words of tongue or pen
The saddest are these: "It might have been!"[80]

The passage of the riders overshadowed the benign "wait-and-see"
attitude of William Wilson's committee, which had examined scientific management and heard Taylor's human-relations-oriented testimony. It had arrived at no condemnation, while the man
responsible for the riders was imperfectly aware of what the system
meant. Yet to much of the public, it must have seemed as if congress had studied and condemned the Taylor system.

The political realities of the rider's passage were clear. Taylor's
theories and officers Wheeler and William's practice were lumped
together as forbidden in defense installations and hence, for at least
part of the public, as equally unwise choices. Taylor's pre-eminent
fear, that his theories and their misapplications might become indis-
tinguishable, became reality in a law that lumped together voluntary and enforced time-and-motion research. The bill's major
impact, then, was not so much its mandate, but rather its implicit
assumption that Taylor's ideas and their use in other people's hands
should be dealt with in only one way and without investigating the
different conditions under which scientific management techniques
might be implemented in organizations. The legislative acceptance
of this assumption was a severe blow to Taylor's attempts to erect a
wall between his proposals and their misapplication, to claim separate intellectual territories for his ideas and for the industrial practices spearheaded by others, particularly industrial practices he had
already explicitly condemned in *Shop Management* and *Principles*.

The Problem of Taylor's Idealism

It is not absurd to call Taylor a scientific managment prophet.
He was so involved in promoting his ideas that his dedication assumes a religious quality, both in its intensity and in its appearance
of proselytizing without financial reward. When the question arose

at the Wilson committee hearings if he had money interests in scientific managment, he responded:

> I have not a cent. I have not accepted any employment money under scientific management of any kind since 1901, and everything I have done in that cause has been done for nothing. I have spent all of the surplus of my income in trying to further the cause for many years past, and am spending it now.[81]

He did not even accept reimbursement for his lectures or travel expenses in discussing scientific management.[82]

A quasi-religious idealism is also present in the optimistic, millenial predictions that more compassionate human behavior would eventually prevail and lead to a better world. Vintage Taylor is his exchange with Rep. William Wilson:

> The Chairman (Wilson.) Mr. Taylor, do you believe that any system of scientific management . . . would revolutionize the minds of the employers to such an extent that they would immediately, voluntarily, and generally enforce the golden rule?
>
> Mr. Taylor. If they had any sense, they would.[83]

In one sense this idealism is Taylor's least attractive feature, because he takes the attitude that misapplication of his ideas on labor-management cooperation is a unique problem rather than a dilemma that happens to many theorists whose work must be applied by others. The idealistic argument for cooperation would also be strengthened if Taylor had related it to his own experience with situations where cooperation was impossible. He knew the thorny road he had walked at Bethlehem Steel. He saw his own associates having petty quarrels.[84] He must have understood the difficulties in gaining cooperation, and yet he embraced it as a realizable ideal, thus limiting the real-world usefulness of his ideas. The most valuable theories on motivation will explain how to create cooperation in a world where thorny paths and petty quarrels are almost the norm.

Miner Chipman, lawyer for the Watertown molders, grasped that idealizing human nature defeated Taylor in his confrontations with practicing managers who borrowed some of his methods. Chipman argues that Taylor "indulged in Utopian dreams equally as panacean as that of the radical socialist." These dreams were bound to fail because they ignored fallen human nature. Chipman notes, "If we were truly righteous, truly just, truly altruistic, if we really loved our brother man, the socialistic commonwealth would not be a bad sort of thing . . . and . . . scientific management would also be a very good thing."[85]

For the real world, Taylor gives too little thought to situations where the impetus for mutually beneficial cooperation coexists with a potential for conflict over how to cooperate (what the political scientist Thomas Schelling calls "mixed-motive" situations).[86] Taylor envisions a future where managers and workers are so closely allied that the need for collective bargaining disappears. Chipman argues:

> It is not for scientific management to build up Utopian conditions, wherein organized labor would be unnecessary. Organized labor IS. It is our job to take it as it is, not as it ought to be, and work out, slowly, if necessary, the conflicting ideals that separate employer and employee.[87]

Towards the end of Taylor's life, University of Chicago economist Robert Hoxie wrote a study also dismissing Taylor as an "idealist" who failed to distinguish between what might be and what actually was.[88] The critique of scientific management as overidealized is borne out in the actual behavior of business managers and government officers. Many of them like Taylor's discrete methods but reject the moral shift that he postulates should accompany these techniques, being skeptical whether their employees are ripe for such conversions.

At the end of the House testimony, Rep. John Tilson asks Taylor, "How many concerns, to your knowledge, use your system in its entirety?" Taylor replies, "In its entirety—none; not one."[89]

Frederick Taylor died of pneumonia on March 21, 1915, bequeathing to his adherents the task of justifying his system, defending it from misinterpretation, and at the same time establishing its practicality by constructing ways of applying it in mixed-motive situations. His disciples informally accepted this challenge by forming the Taylor Society "to preserve, in the midst of a rush of industry to get efficient quickly, the engineering technique and the idealism of what had been given the distinguishing name of scientific management."[90]

Of all Taylor's direct associates, Morris Cooke became most intimately involved in justifying, defending, and applying the system in the public sector. He tries to answer the twin questions: What particular benefits do Taylor's ideas have for public agencies? What are the political consequences of using Taylor's theories? How do the changes they bring to organizations relate to concepts such as managment and worker responsiveness and democratic control? As a man who was a close friend of Taylor and who had a prominent public service career of his own, Cooke bridges the gap between Taylor's ideas on government administration (on which Taylor wrote very little) and the way those ideas are presented in the early political science literature.

In the following chapter we move from examining Taylor's basic theories to analyzing how Cooke applied them to public administration. Cooke's applications can then be compared to mainstream public administration writers' use and criticism of Taylor's theories. Such comparisons allow us to examine the issue of why Taylor's ideas have been used in radically different ways in different historical periods. Why was he an intellectual hero to the discipline in the 1910s and a villain after 1947? How does increasing dependence on the natural science model of understanding a discipline's history relate to this shift in reputation?

Chapter 6

Morris Cooke, a Link between Taylor and Public Administration

In the very years Taylor was working out his management theories, the field of political science was developing as an academic discipline, with public administration under its aegis. After the Civil War, broad, amateur social science interests were represented by the American Social Science Association (1865–1909).[1] But this gave way to a more professional orientation encouraged by the establishment of university departments offering doctoral degrees at Johns Hopkins University in 1876 and Columbia University in 1880.[2] Formation of the American Economic Association (1885), the American Academy of Political and Social Sciences (1889), the American Sociological Association (1903), and the American Political Science Association (APSA) (1903) heralded the growth of social science professions, with officers in each society holding posts in discrete university departments in their specialties. Emulating German models, these departments granted doctorates for mastery of knowledge (what) and research techniques (how); they asserted that scientific study of social phenomena might yield insights not inherent in common sense or received historical practice.

Some idea of the growth of interest in political science as a discipline can be seen in the American Political Science Association's having 214 members in 1904, a year after its founding, 1,350 in 1910.[3] Proliferation of scholarly journals is also indicative of increased support. Columbia University began publishing the *Political Science Quarterly* in 1886; the University of Pennsylvania inaugurated the *Annals of the American Academy of Political and Social Sciences* in 1890; the APSA started the *American Political Science Review* in 1906.

Law, philosophy, and history were the roots of the new discipline. The scientific study of public administration also emanated from attempts by several federal bureaus (e.g., Labor Statistics, the Census) to publish codified material on social conditions, allowing the public to assess and perhaps act on various social patterns.[4]

Frank Goodnow's influential 1900 volume on *Politics and Administration* outlined the new discipline's agenda.[5] The Columbia professor of administrative law argued for supplementing constitutional and historical treatises with analysis of both formal and informal aspects of current political systems. This would uncover how informal and planned relations differ (e.g., why city bosses appear when no statutes call for them) and what ways can make informal patterns conform to formal prescriptions.

A political science that recognizes the difference between planned and unplanned systems and wants to make the latter conform to formal expectations approaches organizational study from a vantage similar to Towne, Halsey, and Taylor's ASME presentations. The engineers asked why all people in factories were not pulling together for maximum productivity as the employers planned. Goodnow asks why the locus of city power is not held by people who are electorally accountable, as state charters mandate.[6] In both cases, answers must be sought through the study of behavior, rather than formal documents. Observation, rather than textual analysis, is the research mode for providing insight into specific and practical techniques for improving political activities.

Political scientists of Goodnow's era had great interest in ASME's management papers. In 1896 the American Economic Association and the Political Science Association of the Central States jointly reprinted in one volume Towne's 1888 paper on gain sharing, Halsey's 1891 premium plan, and Taylor's then hot-off-the-press piece-rate system.[7] Because publication followed so closely on Taylor's presentation, it seems fair to infer that his call for a systematic management science had sparked considerable social science attention to the engineering literature. At a somewhat later date, the *Political Science Quarterly*, edited by Columbia University's government faculty, reviewed *The Principles of Scientific Management*, noting its relevance to understanding and improving city politics.[8]

Taylor never published any articles or books specifically relating his management ideas to public administration, although he had several opportunities to do so. In February 1912, the associate editor of the *Annals* asked for a piece on efficiency in city government, but since Taylor was in Europe and did not think he could make the deadline, he refused.[9] In January 1915, the *Annals* again requested a piece on the subject; Taylor again refused, using the press of other commitments as his excuse.[10]

Two sources give some direct evidence of his perspective on public management. His Watertown Arsenal correspondence shows his understanding of the political parameters within which the public sector manager operates—that in a democracy elected representatives set administrative action's basic parameters and that Congressional perceptions of constituent desires influence federal oversight rules. Before the Arsenal strike, Taylor reminded Crozier that efficiency, narrowly construed, would not lead Congress to support changes so much as would worker satisfaction with the new system expressed at election time.[11] He urged the general to pursue implementation in a way that secured such satisfaction.

At Taylor's death, a manuscript entitled "Government Efficiency" was found among his papers.[12] Despite its sweeping title, the essay only considers the question of personnel selection. As we might expect from a political Progressive, Taylor favors "merit" over spoils systems, which he equates with loafing and fear of change.

Neither of these sources clearly indicate whether Taylor recognized a distinction between the goals of public and private organizations (as did his mentor Metcalfe), or whether such distinctions had any relevance to the use of scientific management in the public sector. They also give us no information on whether Taylor envisioned a special role for scientific management in advancing the Progressive's political agenda.

The closest we can come to approximating Taylor's views on these subjects is by analyzing how one of his closest associates, Morris Cooke, envisioned using scientific management in the political and public sector arena. Cooke makes an attractive link between Taylor—the engineer turned management scholar—and the administrative concerns of people trained in government and public law. Cooke's early education was similar to Taylor's. He held a mechanical engineering bachelor's degree (Lehigh University, 1895); he was active in the ASME, delivering presentations and serving on its National Council. His original interest in Taylor's ideas, around 1903, was to apply them in the publishing industry, where he was an executive. But after 1910 he became concerned almost exclusively with using the principles of scientific management to improve the responsiveness and democratic accountability of public agencies.

His change in orientation is paralleled by a shift in jobs and outlets for his writing. He forged a distinguished public sector executive career, including service as director of Philadelphia's Department of Public Works (1911–1915), director of Pennsylvania's Great Power Survey (1923), chairman of the Public Works Administration's Mississippi Valley Committee (1933), director of the National Resources Board's Water Resources Section (1934) and administrator of the Rural Electrification Administration (1935–1937).[13] Most of his articles after 1910 appear in social science journals such as the *Annals* and the *American Political Science Review*. A 1924 volume he edited on *Public Utility Regulation* contains articles by engineers and a politically anchored piece by Charles Merriam and Harold Lasswell.[14]

Taylor seems to have trusted Cooke's ability to apply shop management. He used Cooke for delicate missions such as briefing Brandeis during the Eastern railroad rate case and for editing and polishing his *Principles*.[15] Taylor recommended Cooke to direct Philadelphia's public works department, a job that both men saw as an opportunity to create a scientific management showcase in the public sector. In November 1911, Rudolph Blankenberg, Philadelphia's reform mayor, asked Taylor to head the department, which employed four thousand people. Taylor refused, suggesting Cooke as an alternative. When Blankenberg hesitated, Taylor pressed the appointment, asserting that Cooke would introduce new ideas because he "stood for the Taylor system." After Mayor Blankenberg agreed, Taylor wrote Cooke, noting, "You . . . accept it with the distinct idea of being able to introduce our methods."[16]

Taylor's trust was not misplaced. Before 1915, Cooke saw his role as carrying out his mentor's principles rather than producing original contributions of his own.[17] After Taylor's death, Cooke assumed the responsibility of monitoring the accuracy of outside assessments of scientific management. He kept up a copious correspondance with Taylor's widow, who asked him to serve on the committee overseeing Copley's authorized biography.[18] He urged her to sue a stockjobbing company that he believed was misusing Taylor's name.[19] His public administration writings often credit Taylor's insights in glowing terms. "Taylor's work . . . has resulted in giving birth to what appears to some of us to be the greatest single force operating for good in the industrial world today."[20]

The close personal relationship is particularly relevant in claiming that Cooke's pre-1916 articles embody Taylor's views, for Cooke showed most of them to his mentor, and sought his criticism. Cooke's writing in this period can be considered to approximate the uses that Taylor himself envisioned for his ideas in public administration. These articles are especially interesting because Cooke does not confine himself to suggesting ways to analyze discrete public tasks to improve their efficiency. He places work analysis in a political framework that explicitly recognizes a difference between public and private goals as well as the primacy of political over administrative considerations in government; he links work analysis to the Progressive cause.

Contrasts abound between Cooke's use of Taylor's insights and the picture of scientific management presented by modern public administration textbooks. They portray an authoritarian, unidimensional system of motivation; Cooke uses a human relations, multidimensional model. They depict scientific management advocates as seeing little difference between public and private organizations and asserting a schematic politics/administration dichotomy. Cooke's work shows that he accepts a distinction between public and private goals and conceives politics and administration as inherently entwined. Students who form their scientific management picture from modern works might be forgiven for wondering if Cooke bases his views on ideas of the same Frederick Taylor they have been hearing about.

Morris Cooke's Scientific Management

Any understanding of Cooke's public sector scientific management has to begin with his concept of public administration. Modern writers assume that advocates of public sector scientific management accepted Woodrow Wilson's axiom that public administration was simply another business field with efficiency the key goal.[21] A recent *Public Administration Review* article observes that "until the 1940s, the study of public administration was little more than the study of efficiency. . . .During that period, the great stress was on economy (doing things at least cost)."[22]

The assumption of Wilsonian influence may occur because the former president is the only 1880s administrative author most modern scholars read, and hence they erroneously assume that he was the major influence on writing about government management at the turn of the century. His actual influence on people supporting the use of Taylor's ideas in public agencies seems nil. No pre-war *American Political Science Review, Annals,* or *Political Science Quarterly* articles on scientific management quote or cite Wilson's essay.

If mechanical engineers such as Taylor or Cooke needed a source on public/private relations, they had easier access to Henry Metcalfe's formulations, presented, in part, at the ASME. This body of work posits a distinction between private management judged on efficiency and government administration evaluated also on legislative accountability.[23] Although Metcalfe's work is almost unknown to modern public administrators, it may have been one source for Cooke's asserting a unique public agency mandate for responsiveness to citizens.

Cooke sees government as a conversion mechanism for public demands.[24] He believes citizen groups should assume the lion's share of setting organizational agendas. Such groups want to accomplish certain ends and use government institutions as a means of implementing the necessary structures and activities. Public agency action does not occur in a vacuum. Groups bring requested changes to the agency's attention. They precipitate action by establishing private models, e.g., parks or kindergartens that eventually win public support, first through adoption by particularly innovative and responsive agencies and then through general public sector acceptance.[25]

Twentieth-century citizen demands emerge at an ever-increasing pace partly because science discovers more ways that organized action benefits people. When biologists learn that typhoid can be water-borne, people demand that cities test and filter the water supply.[26] As local governments (Cooke's primary focus) accept increased responsibility, the need grows to analyze agency work patterns and promote efficiency. Efficiency, for Cooke, is clearly of major importance but it never stands alone as a goal.

Dwight Waldo castigates the early public administration literature for not answering the question, "Efficient for *what?*" He asks, "Is not efficiency for efficiency's sake meaningless? *Is efficiency not necessarily measured in terms of other values?*"[27]

This criticism has no relevance to Cooke, for whom efficiency was no more a primary goal than it had been for Taylor. Taylor prized efficiency as a means to secure bigger profits and hence reach the goal of worker/manager cooperation. Cooke, the public administrator, favored it in government as a means of promoting the unique public sector goal of responsiveness. City agencies need efficiency not because this quality is a good in itself but because they operate in a democracy where the public expects a certain level of service and their responsibility is to meet public demands to the extent possible.[28] Admittedly, Cooke assumed that the early-twentieth-century American public wanted efficiency. He offers no hard evidence that citizens prefer water adequately rather than haphazardly filtered or presentable paving at low cost to shoddy paving at high prices. But he is explicit in noting that where citizens don't mind inefficient services as long as they are inexpensive, no particular merit adheres to efficiency. If citizens value short-term savings to the extent that they will not authorize the expenditures necessary to secure the paving or streetcleaning that is most efficient in the long run, the agency's obligation is to provide the inefficient services citizens desire.[29]

Critics can legitimately fault Cooke for not recognizing the ambiguities inherent in public sector responsiveness. How should agency administrators ascertain the public will? To which public should they respond—voters, organized groups, individuals? What happens when one segment of the public desires one thing and another segment wants the exact opposite? While Cooke gives insufficient attention to these questions, even current public administration analysts (who are much keener on precise definition than commentators of Cooke's generation) have difficulty agreeing on the precise characteristics of a responsive public agency. Cooke is willing to use an amorphous concept of "responsiveness" assuming that the idea has a commonsense core that his audience will recognize.

Scientific management affects responsiveness by offering a plan to operationalize the thrust toward efficiency as a strategy for responding to public demands. Agencies that select first-class people, develop a science or art of work processes, and motivate their personnel should be able to offer substantially equivalent or superior services at lower cost than those that do not. Cooke builds on Taylor's work to provide an early model of public personnel management, whose ultimate worth lies in fostering responsiveness to citizen demands.

Selecting First-Class People

The two selection modes available to Cooke were the spoils system and the civil service model. Following Taylor, Cooke favored a modified civil service system. But while he valued merit, following Taylor's definition, Cooke's criterion for first-class public service personnel was job-related. He shared Taylor's preference for testing on-the-job skills rather than academic knowledge acquired in universities, which created distinct manager/worker categories and made it virtually impossible to promote from within. He was skeptical about written examinations, considering them too theoretical and not likely to be job-related.[30]

To give some scope for informally assessing personality and leadership, he believed department heads should retain some hiring discretion, particularly for bureau chiefs and other higher-level officers. He came under fire from some Progressives for supporting Philadelphia's rule that agency heads could choose any of the top four exam scorers (the "rule-of-four") rather than requiring that the top score be hired as recommended by the Pennsylvania Civil Service Association.[31]

Since he wanted to know whether a given individual had the skills, personality, and morals to perform the job's tasks, not whether he or she had generic intelligence or intellectual ability, Cooke's ideal mode of selection centered on oral tests in which candidates had to solve problems requiring resourcefulness and a sense of ethics. This approach is closer to current assessment center methodologies than to either the spoils system or a doctrinaire insistance on a pristinely objective multiple-choice examination. It relies on Taylor's argument that selection has to be job-related, that a person capable of doing one job well might not live up to the demands of another. While serving as Philadelphia's director of public works, Cooke asked Taylor to select and rate oral tests on leadership ability and an appreciation and regard for beauty in city development.[32] These tests were used to select district surveyers, adding personality qualifications to the requirement that applicants have a knowledge of civil engineering. This accords with Taylor's prescription that the most important qualities for successful leadership are "grit" and "imagination" rather than rote learning.[33] This prescription was the rationale for Cooke's public personnel selection model.

Developing Processes of a Work Science or Art

No other writer in the public administration literature shows Cooke's Taylorite concern for improving efficiency by studying the most mundane tasks and establishing a methodology for doing them well. While most writers on urban issues concentrate on police or schools, Cooke's 1918 book discusses the science of street paving; an ASME paper analyzes snow-removal techniques.[34] These activities, which seem hopelessly routine, do matter to people. Efficient paving or snow removal can be a way of being responsive. In the 1960s, a poor snow removal job in the Borough of Queens helped cost a New York City mayor his political career![35]

Taylor had to defend himself against charges that job analysis stifled worker initiative. Cooke is explicit in envisioning a participative process in which workers learn the planning room's methods and then suggest improvements. Experiments are done to see whose techniques allow a greater day's work. The best street paver's methods becomes the standard accepted for all if they produce better results.[36]

Cooke also tackles the question of the expert's role in a public agency. Some modern public administration writers argue that scientific management's adherents wanted experts on top rather than on tap, that they believed experts could run the government better than democratically elected representatives.[37] Such an idea would have appalled Cooke. For him, the recommendations of the work analysis expert are useless unless the public has confidence in them. If the people object to a new technique, "over the side it goes—perhaps never to return."[38] Administrators who want to run efficient agencies have to go out of their way to explain to the public why they are hiring work analysis experts and how their activities help satisfy public expectations. Experts have to report their results in language that the general population understands. Cooke, who wrote a jargon-free prose, was fond of quoting Lord Kelvin's remark that a physicist should be able to explain any new process to the man on the street, arguing that the same should be true of the public sector engineer. Cooke's preferred political universe does not include experts ruling by fiat. It includes work analysis experts explaining their methods to the public and seeking support from legislators for their activities.[39] Rather than seeking to professionalize politics, Cooke strove to democratize expertise by forcing the public sector engineer to put his ideas up for acceptance or disapproval by the interested public.

However, the weakness of this approach lies in Cooke's nebulous treatment of how the public can register opinions. He pays little attention to time constraints on the average citizen, leaving him or her little energy to act on administrative questions. Cooke is following Taylor's psychological predisposition in idealizing reality when he asserts that in a democracy expertise ceases to be a "highbrow" activity as professionals explain their findings to the public and proceed only when their recommendations accord with citizen desires.[40]

Because Cooke envisions frequent, direct expert/public communication, he sees the supposedly neutral professional as inevitably enmeshed in the political process. Cooke's vision undermines the common assertion that pre-World-War-II public administration writers dichotomized politics and administration, favoring structures to isolate agency personnel from the political process.[41] As a practicing agency executive, he was well aware that senior administrators cannot avoid shaping policy. He calls city managers "politicians." He argues that engineers doing governmental work analysis cannot avoid a political role because they have to explain their ideas to the public and elected officials; constant, sustained, two-way conversation with public and officials is a political activity.[42] Cooke never worked out a formal model of the relative roles of legislators and bureaucrats in dialog with the public or the role for a bureaucrat who thinks the citizens are saying one thing while the legislators believe citizens are asking for something very different. Lack of attention to such questions gives his view a fuzzy, vague quality. But this problem is different from placing administrators and experts outside the political process.

Motivating Personnel

Cooke emphasizes a multiple motivations approach that the current public administration literature rarely associates with scientific management. Since he could not use wage incentives in Philadelphia, his 1911–1915 articles and speeches make little reference to economic motivation, a point that does not seem to have troubled Taylor, who reviewed most of them. Taylor was not slow to disavow what he considered misguided attempts to apply his system but expressed no disapproval of Cooke's centering all his motivation efforts on noneconomic factors. Contrary to the argument of modern public administration textbooks, Taylor was quick to disavow people like Wheeler and Williams who omitted voluntary participation, but he willingly lent his name as mentor to Cooke's effort to bring job-related selection, work analysis, communication, and training to Philadelphia—even if the system had to operate without wage incentives.

Prior to 1920, Cooke advocated motivational strategies that most modern public administration writers attribute to books published in the 1930s or later. Cooke foreshadows insights currently associated with the Hawthorne group, Douglas McGregor, Abraham Maslow, and Chester Barnard. Cooke's suggestions often simply reinforce or extend Taylor's own insights. Let us examine some of these foreshadowings of modern theories of motivation.

Hawthorne

A current organization theory text by Michael Harmon and Richard Mayer labels the Hawthorne researchers as the first to note a connection between morale and efficiency, a relationship the scientific management advocates "failed to take adequate account of."[43] The textbook writers do not seem to have read much Cooke. Years before Hawthorne, he laments that so many managers share "the mistaken idea that the man at the top is in a position to tell the man at the bottom what is good for him."[44] Cooke prefers to see agencies "run by the collective intelligence of the many."[45]

The organization theory text attributes to the Hawthorne writers the insight that employee complaints and lower morale may stem from personal off-the-job problems.[46] To improve productivity, a supervisor has to be close enough to the workers to understand their private lives. This insight hardly originates at Hawthorne. In a 1913 paper, Cooke asserts, "Nine times out of ten you will find a sick child or wife at home, the worker in debt, or some other purely personal reason for work below par."[47] He urges casual and even intimate supervisor/worker conversations to learn how personal conflicts affect performance. But the insight does not originate with Cooke. Taylor himself writes:

> Workers must be in a happy frame of mind to be efficient. . . . Many of them have troubles at home with which they are unable to cope single handed. Whatever they are, in their remedy lies the change in point of view.[48]

This is the source of Cooke's view. When F. J. Roethlisberger and William Dickson conceive a need to know worker sentiments, they are reinforcing scientific management rather than inventing a new theory of motivation. This leaves the questions: Why do current texts present these insights as new-minted in 1939? Why is Cooke's paper never mentioned? Is the actual thrust of the early literature distorted to accord with the natural science model of steady progress in disciplines over time?

Work as Motivator

The Hawthorne studies advocate improving the context of work. When modern public administration texts want to show that it is work itself that motivates, they refer to theories of Douglas McGregor or Abraham Maslow. McGregor's Theory Y is a set of assumptions, that (1) work is as natural as sleep or play, and (2) the accomplishing of challenging, responsible tasks can motivate employees without reference to the money or pleasant surroundings in employment.[49] Maslow's "self-actualization" concept refers to people who are "devoted, working at something, something which is very precious to them—some calling or vocation . . . which they love, so that the work-joy dichotomy in them disappears."[50]

Theory Y and self-actualization are concepts from the 1950s. If textbooks wanted an earlier source, they could have quoted Cooke's 1917 article that asserts the most important management function to be establishing training that lets employees motivate themselves with the prospect of higher-level and more interesting work.[51] Organizational improvement:

> will always be ineffectually done if it is confined to well-educated and highly trained men at the top. . . . Administrative leadership will in the future more and more consist in getting the largest possible number "into the play" in having the great body of employees increasingly critical in their judgments about their own work and the work which is going on around them.[52]

But this "cannot be brought about unless the worker is inspired with joy in his task."[53] Even the very unbureaucratic association of work and joy, which some readers find so startling in Maslow, appeared first in Cooke's invocation to the task-motivated employee!

Again, Taylor provides much of the basis for Cooke's ideas. The stress on training and development appears in Taylor's *Shop Management* and *Principles*. The notion that manual work is worth doing well dominates scientific management. The worker who uses efficient methods is described as adopting "a pace under which men become happier."[54] Cooke simply gives this aspect of Taylor's thought greater prominence.

Bottom-up Authority

Modern public administration textbooks often credit Chester I. Barnard with originating a bottom-up concept of authority. The assumption seems to be that before Barnard's 1938 reformulation theorists assumed authority was delegated from the top down, and that it was Barnard who originated the idea that subordinates accept orders only when they understand them, believe them consistent with the organization's purpose, and are willing to comply.[55] Managers cannot assume that obedience flows from their high hierarchical status; they must develop leadership skills, including the ability to persuade workers and offer them appropriate incentives.

The idea that pre-1938 managers assumed that workers followed orders is negated by every ASME discussion on the topic. The notion that managers cannot depend on their hierarchical status is not one that Taylor had to develop. His 1880s predecessors were desperately trying to find substitute mechanisms to compel performance. Cooke simply restates a well-known quandary: "We work on the fiction that an instruction once issued is carried out to the letter."[56] Predating Barnard's book by over twenty years, he notes that orders are often misunderstood and that if no one follows them then no leadership exists. His advice is never to give orders as such but rather to convince employees—with the proviso, that if they can convince you of an alternative, so much the better.

Whereas Barnard stresses the value of personal leadership, Cooke articulates the essential scientific management preference for linking obedience and information. In his scenario, employees are expected to accept the administrator who has the requisite knowledge rather than the one who fits the correct slot on the hierarchy. Orders become instructions. The supervisor, in effect, urges employees to follow his strategies because he knows how to reach a given end. This involves nurturing Barnard-style leadership ability to persuade employees or allow them to convince the supervisor of the superiority of their own methods. With information rather than authority as the key to acceptance, communication ability assumes an importance utterly lacking in the conventional top-down picture.

Cooke's theory can fill the textbook attributions currently assigned to Barnard. Again, the question is: Why do all well-known textbook authors choose to ignore Cooke's articles and attribute the discovery of what are in fact his ideas to later writers? Why do textbooks portray ideas Cooke actually considered essential to scientific management as a repudiation of what they describe as his theory's narrow outlook?

If Cooke were alive today, the question would still have scholarly as well as personal relevance for him because of his concern with distortion and misappropriation of information. In his own sphere he was trying to understand the social biasses affecting information exchange. He assigned such exchange a crucial role in public administration. It was part of careful selection, work analysis, motivation, and agency-citizen interactions. In one speech he asks rhetorically, "Can there be genuine democracy where there is lack of publicity?" and answers with a hearty negative.[57] The job of the agency executive is to publicize his rationale to the citizens at large. The job of the supervisor is to explain his rationale to employees. Persuasion is the key to internal efficiency. The internal importance of communication mirrors its wider political role. The crucial political activities are acquiring information, sharing it with the public, and providing channels for the public to use this information to influence the agendas that agencies pursue. Communication's internal importance emerges from the new obligations scientific management imposes on supervisors. Its political role also emerges from scientific management and will be examined in the following section.

The Role of Information

For Taylor, information was the key to factory reform. As early as 1895 he insisted that the uniqueness of his approach lay in bringing new data to solve old problems. Without work analysis to cut the time taken to produce a given unit of output, managers could not solve the high-wages/high-labor-costs conundrum. Add new information on work and the problem might be solved.

Cooke is very much in the scientific management tradition in seeing information as the key to municipal reform. As a Progressive he believed too many cities languished under the rule of corrupt machines allied to special interests. He particularly criticized the alliance with utilities, which he believed often underserved and overcharged their cities for light, gas, and water. While some Progressives advocated municipal ownership of utilities, Cooke argued this take-over was premature. In the 1911–1915 period, no one could know which legal arrangements would facilitate reform because data for feasible standards were lacking.[58] Without information on comparative performance or what experts said could be done to improve conditions, voters had little to guide them in responding to skewed utility prices. Once there was more data available, citizen groups could make their agenda for change known for government response.[59]

During and immediately after his Philadelphia tenure, Cooke tried to amass utility performance information, because its absence was a resource to maintain the status quo. He sought data (1) relating actual performance to contract specifications and (2) suggesting fair standards—the municipal utility equivalent of Taylor's fair day's work. How much should a city pay a well-run electric company—three cents per kilowatt hour, five cents, ten? Until people could answer this question, debates on price restructuring were premature.

From a technical standpoint, information on utility performance was fairly easy to obtain, although Cooke found that his predecessors in Philadelphia had not displayed much interest in getting it. When he became Philadelphia's public works director, the Welsbach Street Lighting Company held a contract to furnish the city with street lamps giving a minimum of sixty candle power.[60] Although the company had held the contract for thirty-four years, no one had obtained an independent check on whether Welsbach actually met its obligations. Believing that the company should not be allowed to charge for sixty candle power unless it provided that amount, Cooke asked New York's Electric Testing Laboratories to check whether the lamps met contract standards. The verdict was that only 75% of the obligatory candlepower was delivered in January 1913. The city decided to fine Welsbach about ten thousand dollars, proof for Cooke that data collection and "publicity—incessant and relentless"[61] could influence utility politicies, a phenomen he calls "a very remarkable outcome of the scientific management movement."[62]

Welsbach's dereliction was relatively easy to prove with tests relating actual performance to contracts. More difficult was deciding how to word new contracts. To give efficient service to Philadelphians, Cooke needed comparative figures on electric and gas costs and the valuation of utilities' assets. To see what information was available, Cooke planned a 1914 conference on utility policy, "so arranged as to give opportunity for a fair hearing to all the interests at stake—capital, labor, the public official, the consumer."[63]

Characteristically, he cleared the idea first with Taylor,[64] and then sought prominent political and academic support. Although he conceived and coordinated the entire conference, he arranged for it to be held under the American Academy of Political and Social Science's imprimature, and hosted by five reform-oriented mayors—his own Mayor Rudolph Blankenberg, John Purroy Mitchel (New York), Carter Harrison (Chicago), Newton Baker (Cleveland), and George Shroyer (Dayton). Panels mingled political figures with university political scientists (e.g., Mitchel and Charles Merriam).

Before the conference opened on November 12, Cooke hoped it would endorse a National Bureau of Utilities Research funded by interested cities to exchange data. Throughout the summer, Cooke did the spadework for this organization, soliciting Taylor and Brandeis' permission to use their names on a Board of Trustees,[65] and urging the five reform mayors to provide money. He argued that information was a prerequisite to resolving political problems[66] (even though his use of data against Welsbach had earned him assorted personal threats[67]).

November 1914 brought agreement by the mayors to inaugurate a Bureau with Cooke as director. He moved from line management to a position centering on amassing politically sensitive data on utility rates and service standards, information he believed would remove most excuse for conflict between the public and the utility companies. Cooke inherited some of Taylor's idealism, a phenomenon that becomes apparent—and problematic—when he asked the utilities trade association to share data with the Bureau. He quickly learned that the utility companies would not share their information even if a third party (such as Cooke) argued that this would lead to a resolution of quarrels between the public and the utilities' corporations.

The Utilities Battle

The problem Cooke faced at the Bureau of Utilities Research was similar, in theory, to the tension dogging Taylor's footsteps from Bethlehem to the Watertown Arsenal. The status quo was threatened by newcomers armed with data; groups keen on preserving things as they were had every reason to thwart collection of new facts. Both managers and workers tried to stop Taylor when they preferred the status quo to the changes they imagined his work producing. Utilities and their allies proved unlikely to aid Cooke's attempt to amass information on electric and gas production.

The difference was that as a consultant, Taylor worked under the aegis of a company's authority, limiting the obstacles that supervisors or individual workers could put in his path. No authority obliged the utilities to cooperate with Cooke's Bureau. Trade organizations such as the National Electric Light Association flatly refused to share data.[68]

Lack of access forced Cooke to confront communications' social dimension. He had to recognize how much information exchange depends on incentive structures—who interacts with whom, who is willing and able to pass data beyond an organization's boundaries.

As in so many other corporate areas, he who pays the piper seems to call the tune. The best experts were retained as consultants by the utility companies. When Cooke tried to hire engineers, he found the most prominent were unable to work for his organization. Their information was locked into company reports rather than available to the public.

In a set of lectures delivered at Eastern universities early in 1915, Cooke blasted four extremely prominent engineers who served as utility consultants.[69] The crux of the indictment was that they had overvalued corporate assets in briefs they had prepared for state Public Service Commissioners and which were used to determine utility rates—and that they had done this because it was in the interest of the companies paying their fees.

The engineers responded by labeling Cooke's behavior "unprofessional." Instead of countering his accusations directly, they asked the ASME to censure him because he had cast aspersions on their reputations before lay audiences, in forums where they were absent and not in a position to counter the charges. Specifically, they accused him of violating the ASME's Ethics Code directing professionals to "endeavor to protect all reputable engineers from misrepresentation" and to "be broad and generous, with the facts plainly stated."[70]

Here was an issue pitting the public's right to know against professional and industrial norms of silence. The four consultants presupposed that professionals share guild interests; each helps the others, each is obligated to moderate criticism in addressing the public. This view goes far beyond the universal onus against bearing false witness. It mandates withholding perceived truth that tends to be caustic or disparaging, and dispensing some criticisms only in narrow professional settings.

This view is totally at variance with Cooke's credo that a public sector expert's primary responsibility is to give the public as much relevant information as possible. With some acerbity, he writes the chair of ASME's ethics committee:

> Your letter dated December 22d, marked "Personal and Confidential," has been received. My contact with the matter of complaint . . . has to do with my public position. There is nothing in connection with it that cannot and should not be open to the public. I have never written personal and confidential letters in regard to public business. I think you will agree that this is a good rule for any public official to follow. Correspondence forms a part of a public official's record and should on both sides be available to the public. . . . I believe it to be against the public interest for engineers or any other professional group to thrash out questions like this except with the widest and freest discussion and the broadest opportunity for present and ultimate publicity.[71]

To ASME's secretary, he inveighs:

> The comments I made on their views did not go beyond such relations to purely public matters as are inherent in the public or semi-public positions each has held. Their technical engineering ability was not questioned.[72]

Why then should he be restricted to technical settings?

At the time of this dispute Cooke was hardly an ASME outsider, having served on its Council in 1914. Nevertheless, the committee voted to censure him alleging that Cooke had violated professional norms by taking his complaints to a public forum. Cooke responded by indicating his intention to write a pamphlet giving his side of the case and distributing it to ASME members.

While he was preparing this piece, he received an invitation to participate in a panel on utilities scheduled for ASME's 1917 meeting in Boston. Delighted at an additional opportunity to present his views, he accepted—whereupon the invitation was withdrawn. The panel chair explained that he wanted a more restricted session; Cooke, however, alleged electric company pressure.[73]

The panel turnaround brought to the fore the futility of ASME's charter provision forbidding any discussion of political issues. This provision had prevented any sessions on the Dietrick Amendment.[74] But as soon as the political question was whether to publicize relations with utilities, the notion of silence as strict neutrality fell apart. What could the provision mean in relation to the utilities battle? Any ASME action was likely to have some kind of political effect; both allowing and disallowing Cooke's presentation were actions fraught with political overtones. The pamphlet Cooke wrote protesting the ethics committee censure opens with a denunciation of the Society for considering political discussions "prejudicial" to its interests and notes that, "When we describe politics as 'the science of government,' . . . it is only too clear that our profession cannot evade . . . an active part."[75]

Modern textbooks tend to portray scientific management as an apolitical administrative theory. Their authors might be surprised to learn that Cooke's stance against the possibility of a nonpolitical engineering professional society he saw as an outgrowth of applying scientific management principles to improving municipal efficiency. The idea that politics could not be avoided in discussions of municipal engineering also received Taylor's backing; Cooke's correspondence strongly suggests that the younger man sought his mentor's advice in every stage of the battle right up to Taylor's death in March 1915. Cooke notes, "No man every [sic] received stronger or more consistent support in the performance of disagreeable duties than I received from Mr. Taylor. Especially as to utility conditions we understood each other perfectly."[76]

Cooke's fight to increase the information available to the lay public builds (whether consciously or unconsciously) on Taylor's decision to publish *Principles* in a popular magazine, one with strong political attachments (where it was accepted as a piece calling for insurgency). Both men insist that information others want to restrict actually belongs to a larger public. Operating in a government organization, Cooke makes the additional point that widespread information dissemination is necessary to maintain public agency responsiveness and accountability. He also displays greater sophistication about the social and political biasses lurking in supposedly neutral information. A case in point is his criticism of law reports. Most people would probably label reports publishing court decisions as bias-free. Cooke argues that some of the reports are financially indebted to utilities magnates and devote more space to decisions favorable to their sponsors. Although the reports print no lies, he perceives their space allotments as creating a dangerous propaganda. People think they receive an accurate picture of judicial decisions while actually getting an ideologically skewed version through the placement of decisions and the number of lines allotted to each.[77]

For Cooke, the key to scientific management is the quest for information. Because information is such a crucial variable, its distribution inevitably becomes the focus of political battles. Those who possess it are drawn into the political fray. No concrete wall separates politics and administrators, nor could it separate them, because one aspect of politics is controversy over distributing the knowledge held by administrative experts. Cooke's administrative career is an object lesson in how the committed public sector professional has to get involved in planning distribution channels—deciding how, where, and when to release information, so that citizens have accessible, understandable data necessary to participate in the political process. The Progressive Cooke hardly sees such administrative decisions as apolitical. He is quite aware that some distribution channels favor one group of interests, while other channels give an edge to those interests' opponents. The scientific management advocate in government is always involved in politics—and is understood by Cooke to have such an involvement.

Although Cooke is rarely if ever cited in contemporary public administration literature, his views on scientific management accord with dominant tendencies in the discipline prior to the late 1940s. Many political scientists of his era saw Taylor's primary contribution as defining as researchable activities that people had previously thought unworthy of study. A new dispensation was in the air to ferret out and publicize facts about the public business. The quest for information was fueled by its promise of changing political realities; information was seen as a resource for creating more responsive agencies.

This approach is particularly apparent in works associated with the New York Bureau of Municipal Research, an organization dominated by the public administration advocates who had the closest personal contact with Taylor and his circle. It also governs the treatment of scientific management in textbooks of the 1920s and 1930s.

The next chapter analyzes the Bureau's works that share at least two traits with Cooke's output. They stress the same part of Taylor's message. When not simply ignored, their insights are denigrated in the modern literature. The tendency is to ignore Cooke and to treat the Bureau literature as more naive than careful reading shows it to be.

Chapter 7

Scientific Management and Public Administration: Act One

The origin of the New York Bureau of Municipal Research (BMR) has been equated with the founding of the discipline of public administration because it typifies an early application of Frederick Taylor's quest for information to city affairs.[1] The incorporation of the Bureau represents the first attempt to deliberately organize and compare techniques for accomplishing municipal work to help agencies perform tasks more expeditiously and give citizens the data needed to maintain control over their government. Charles Goodsell calls the organization itself "a mecca and a model for governmental reform for the entire country."[2]

In 1906 Dr. William H. Allen, general agent for the Association for Improving the Condition of the Poor (AICP), approached a group of New York philanthropists, including Andrew Carnegie and John D. Rockefeller, to fund a bureau to develop and disseminate city government performance information.[3] Incorporated in May 1907, the organization worked under the assumption that such data had a role to play in municipal reform. As Allen has noted:

> Our key idea in starting continuous municipal research was that attacking men as criminals and looking for crime in government . . . gave little if any protection at all to the public. If there really was to be better government, the public must know how governing was done and must help those in power use better methods.[4]

The four Bureau officials whose thought this chapter analyzes are Allen, Henry Bruere, Charles A. Beard, and Frederick Cleveland. Allen, Bruere, and Cleveland, sometimes dubbed "the ABC powers,"[5] were its senior administrators from its inception. Beard became director of the BMR Training School for Public Service in 1917.

Both Bruere and Cleveland had pre-Bureau connections with Allen. Bruere, a Harvard Law School graduate, had performed AICP investigations under Allen's tutelage. Cleveland, a professor at New York University's School of Commerce, had met Allen when both were studying for their doctorate in political science and economics at the University of Pennsylvania.

While Beard is principally known for his economic interpretation of the constitution,[6] he held a 1904 Columbia University Ph.D. in public law and government, and taught in the same department as Frank Goodnow before joining Allen's team. He was President of the American Political Science Association in 1926, and active in founding the American Society for Public Administration.

Of the four men, Cleveland had the closest personal relations with Taylor and his circle. Morris Cooke, in particular, was instrumental in bringing Cleveland and Taylor together. He invited both to speak at a 1912 scientific management conference he organized at Dartmouth College. (Cleveland discussed how to adapt Taylor's ideas to city governments, without, it seems, provoking any disagreement from Taylor.[7]) Cooke selected both men for the Board of Trustees of the National Bureau of Utilities Research.[8] Cleveland and Cooke exchanged correspondence at least into the 1920s, each sending the other scholarly articles and personal anecdotes.[9] Cleveland's clear connection with scientific management's inner circle may have been one reason President William Howard Taft appointed him chairman of the 1911 national Commission on Economy and Efficiency.

No comparable personal connection can be established between the other BMR adminstrators and Taylor's personal circle. However, the idea of intervening in organizational outcomes through fact gathering and analysis appealed to all of them because they believed cities faced a situation similar to the one that had confronted Taylor at Midvale over twenty years previously. Little information existed on managing urban operations. Comparative analysis, systematic weighing of the benefits of one city program against another, was almost nonexistent. In 1904 the New York City Board of Education announced curtailment of summer and night schools for lack of funds.[10] Civic groups asked to see records on how the Board's money was being spent; could other economies be made and these programs kept? According to officials of the New York Committee on Physical Welfare for School Children no one knew; no records along these dimensions were kept in a form easily available to the public.

As optimists and idealists, the BMR triumverate saw this type of information as a powerful weapon in the struggle for popular control of government. Without sufficient data, the public was powerless to hold elected officials accountable. Such officials lacked the information to supervise the bureaucracies. Determined Taylor-style analysis of administrative operations would give the public comparative data on how other cities balanced their budgets and whether it should accept its own level of public health services, education retention rates, prison recidivism, or water charges. It would show the best available administrative techniques allowing people to "get done what all the time they had wanted to get done but didn't know how to do."[11]

Taylor's primary lesson for Allen and his associates was his implicit assumption that questions of organizational planning and implementation are researchable, that information collection and use is both possible and salutory for future performance. The underlying rationale for Taylor's work is that research-based intervention has positive performance consequences, that knowledge gained through specific experiments can be used to alter day-by-day production realities. Bureau research accepts this assumption as its most basic premise, positing that in the public sector the consequences have two dimensions. At the administrative level, data affect executive/employee relations, since departments can select and promote personnel on the basis of job-related skills rather than seniority and written test performance.[12] At the political level, a shift occurs in the way elected executives, legislators, and particularly the citizenry at large relate to public agencies.

Several times in American history, a shift has occurred in the consensus on the problems best handled by private and those by public action.[13] The first two decades of the twentieth century saw such a period of ferment. The BMR shared the basic Progressive inclination to increase the scope of state and local government action. Bureau officials argued that city governments should assume charitable and health functions previously reserved for private associations; they wanted public administrators authorized to regulate such things as child labor and loan transactions in factories and banks previously exempt from state surveillance.[14]

Irresponsible government was seen as an impediment to such change. Cleveland argues that the public will not support extension of control by informal cabals run by bosses, those "designing few who look upon government as an institution which they can use to grind their own grist."[15] Why should citizens do so, Bruere asks, as long as they

> are kept at arm's length from city government by roundabout ways of nominating candidates, cumbersome and complicated election laws, multiplicity of elective officials *and the absence of current publication of facts regarding public business* (emphasis in the original)?[16]

First an effective mechanism of popular control must be devised; then the people will consent to further developing state power.[17]

Collecting and disseminating information is offered as the instrument of control. It creates a situation where "democracy does not merely mean periodical elections. It means a government held accountable to the people between elections."[18] When citizens have data on how government jobs are and might be done then they will be able to play a larger role in guiding government actions; this sense of control will change their consensus on what the state should be allowed to do.

Like Cooke, the Bureau founders see Taylor's contribution as profoundly political in its public sector implications. Collecting performance information is not valued simply as an administrative technique but rather because it links citizens and policy, enabling people to register intelligent preferences both during and between elections. To the BMR writers, scientific management is far from nonpolitical in its most global, long-range consequences. It is embraced precisely because of the way it is deemed likely to change citizen participation in urban politics.

Unrealistic Expectations

Bureau researchers can be faulted on at least two counts of naivete. First, they were overoptimistic about human nature, imagining that a few reports will make turn-of-the-century New York resemble the most utopian picture of Athenian democracy. Much too little attention is given to time constraints on the average citizens, leaving them little energy, and perhaps even inclination to absorb and act on whatever performance information is available.

Allen makes several references to the need to keep data intelligible,[19] but the general assumption is that performance information can be given to the average citizens in a form that will make their interest in street paving or milk inspection as strong as the BMR researcher's. Little attention is given to the impact of selective exposure, perception, and retention (not to mention surfeit or boredom) as brakes on the general public's willingness to plow through the information the Bureau was collecting.

This should not suggest that information has no political impact. Some city officials saw the Bureau's collection efforts as a threat. One Borough President refused Bruere permission to see construction records that were legally available to the public.[20] In 1918, Mayor John Hylan closed all city records to BMR employees.[21] But a difference exists between anticipating an attentive audience for disclosures of corruption or boondoggle and expecting, along with Beard, that new data would result in a mass public "maintaining a constant and discriminating scrutiny over public authorities all the year round."[22] The first prediction is likely, the second, unrealistic (or even dismal, if the idea of a public constantly glued on admininstrative detail sounds too joyless).

A second element of unsophistication relates to funding, particularly people's willingness to pay now for long-range goals. As was the case with Taylor, Bureau researchers gravitated to the long view. Since investment in data collection seemed likely to bring future benefits, they assumed that philanthropists would fund it. If studies show new techniques improve sanitation or police work, they assumed that cities would find the resources to train employees or purchase more up-to-date, standardized equipment. They had no patience with or understanding of hesitancy to spend money today for benefits that may (or may not) come sometime in the future.

The tendency in modern references to the Bureau's work is to go beyond noting these endemic problems to portray the municipal reform literature as consistently more constricted in outlook and less political than it is. As with Taylor and Cooke's work, the Bureau is denied credit for insights in its publications. Comparing the accusations against municipal reform to excerpts from actual Bureau work gives further evidence for a split between substance and reputation in the post-World-War-II handling of these earlier scholarly contributions. This divergence is clearly visible in the four criticisms by Dwight Waldo discussed in Chapter 1, used by some recent authors to disparage the sophistication of their predecessor's work.

Bureau reports are criticized for not understanding a public/private-sector dichotomy, setting efficiency as a paramount goal, relying on the primacy of facts rather than paradigms, and minimizing the need for more workplace democracy. How accurate are these charges? None captures the complexities of Bureau thought. In some cases the thrust of BMR literature is diametrically opposed to that assigned it by modern summaries. In other cases, at least one Bureau writer takes a more sophisticated stance than that claimed as typical of his colleagues. Let us compare each criticism to Bureau publications.

The Public-/Private-Sector Dichotomy

One criticism claims indiscriminate borrowing of business concepts by the Bureau of Municipal Research without considering whether they are applicable to the public sphere.[23] This charge assumes that turn-of-the-century scholars understand government management as simply another business field; what worked at Bethlehem Steel was bound to work in New York City agencies.

The question of any congruence between business and public administration is considered a uniquely modern preoccupation. The literature since World War II debates whether public and business management are so different that the idea flow between their disciplines is limited. Some scholars hold with Wallace Sayre's aphorism that public and private are alike in all unimportant matters.[24] On the other hand, others approve Howard McCurdy's thesis that "a fairly straightforward business management approach is probably appropriate for a large number of government activities."[25] Whatever view recent public administration specialists take, however, their underlying assumption is that debating this subject is relatively new, that it represents a challenge to unexamined earlier belief in congruity between the business and the public sectors.

This attitude cannot survive a literature search. The public/private dichotomy was an object of debate prior to World War I. A 1914 *Political Science Quarterly* article on the scientific management of employment offices dissects similarities and differences between public and private employment agencies. The author argues that to be effective, both have to find jobs for clients, but that a public agency has the additional responsibility of studying the causes for unemployment and ameliorating them. He concludes that despite broader goals, public organizations can benefit from certain private sector techniques, particularly better record keeping and the use of training and of career ladders.[26] The point that should be stressed is that the author does not simply assume that such techniques are applicable. He examines the similarities and differences in the two sectors and then makes a specific judgment for a particular case.

A 1917 *American Political Science Review* article argues that the functions of government and business are very different, and therefore their processes must also vary. Business exists for profit while the goal of democratic government is to help the people accomplish their collective desires. While corporations fear too much internal democracy, the proper way to run a government is with open, drawn-out procedures.[27]

No doubt exists that Bureau writers borrowed scientific management from a factory context. They believed techniques pioneered by Taylor would supercede traditional public sector planning methods and this change would benefit the polity. Bruere boasts that "city after city is discarding the old political makeshifts of public administration to adopt business methods in imitation of private enterprise."[28] But they did not borrow the methods without giving attention to how they had to be adapted to the unique goals of a public system.

That theirs was not haphazard, unsophisticated borrowing can be seen in the outline for a course that Allen, Bruere, and Cleveland gave at Columbia University in the spring of 1909.[29] The syllabus contains three sections. The first, "Principles of Public Administration," focuses on similarities and differences between public and private organizations. Here administration is linked to politics by participants discussing the relation of data collection to executive, legislative, and electoral control of bureaucracies, including Progressive-sponsored innovations such as petition, initiative, referendum, and recall.

The second part of the course concentrates on organizations that influence the public administrator. These include other federal, state, and local agencies as well as volunteer groups such as religious organizations and taxpayer associations. The course also considers the political and managerial significance of the citizen's right to inspect public papers.

The third section discusses borrowing business methods for public administration. No a priori assumption is made that public agencies should automatically borrow all the latest private innovations. The students were to study whether agencies should centralize staff functions, a new innovation in private firms. The course discusses what municipalities can learn from private enterprise experience with debt financing, such as floating short- and long-term bonds.

This course does not appear to be a series of how-to lessons designed to encourage wholesale, indiscriminate borrowing of private sector techniques. The decision to use particular business methods in government has to fit into the framework established in the first section on their differences, just as present-day public administrators have to decide whether to borrow private firm use of computers or other new technologies.

Allen explicitly states that the use of scientific management techniques has a unique rationale in the public sector. Private firms may use them solely to promote efficiency. Their prime use in government is to provide data for the public to use in monitoring methods, actions, and results.[30] Effective borrowing of private firms' techniques turns business strategms into political weapons that allow the community to find out and make known whether agencies are meeting its needs. The use of scientific management is given an explicitly political rationale based on an understanding of underlying public/private differences in methods of control and distribution of benefits.[31] For public sector purposes, it is linked with the possibility of increased responsiveness. For Bureau writers, this political goal requires borrowing scientific management; while one can quarrel with the linkage, one cannot legitimately argue that the appropriation took place without reference to unique political needs. A public/private goal dichotomy is recognized as a frame for such appropriations.

Efficiency and Responsiveness

A second criticism stems from a serious misreading of Bureau discussion of efficiency. Bureau writers accord this concept respect. Allen's *Efficient Democracy* opens with the provocative statement that efficiency is more important than uniformed goodness,[32] and continues with chapters labeled "Hospital Efficiency," "School Efficiency," "Efficiency in Charitable Work," etc.

This appreciation is misread by many modern writers as homage to efficiency as an ultimate goal. Dwight Waldo was the first to criticize the municipal reform literature for this, noting correctly that efficiency cannot actually serve as an aim in itself; actions are never simply efficient or inefficient but are one or the other for some other purpose.[33]

Although the charge is now part of what everyone in the discipline knows, it is in fact misplaced in regard to Bureau literature, as it is for Taylor and Cooke's assertions: For Bureau writers, efficiency is a strategy. In one pamphlet, Bruere describes a police agency's goal as "to accomplish efficiently the purpose for which it is maintained."[34] Cleveland notes that:

> The demand for efficiency must go farther than to . . . get a dollar for every dollar spent; it must constitute a demand that the government is doing the thing most needed, is conserving those ends and purposes which cannot be adequately reached through private undertakings.[35]

These sentences make plain that efficiency does not stand alone as a goal but is a way of achieving some further purpose.

Bureau literature accords respect to efficiency as a strategy for increasing government responsiveness. Modern writers tend to define efficiency as accomplishing a given task with most effect at least expenditure. The Bureau generation used a different definition. In a 1912 article, William Prendergast, New York City's comptroller, openly rejected an American Society for Promoting Efficiency definition of "results/expenditures." For cities, he preferred to define efficiency as doing those activities that the public wants done as well as possible at the least expense, a wording that makes explicit that efficient action requires agency responsiveness to public desires.[36] Bruere insists on differentiating his own intentions from the way builders use efficiency. New York's East River bridges may be a marvel of efficiency to construction engineers but Bruere considers them an example of inefficiency because the planners did not consider how to design the structures with the needs of mass transit passengers, and so the bridges are not responsive to this population's needs.[37] A modern political scientist would be likely to say the bridges were efficiently constructed but unresponsive to the community; Bruere simply calls them inefficient.

The modern writer often links efficiency with order and precision, but Bruere reminds his readers that:

> To be progressively efficient, municipal service must be based upon a complete and continuing understanding of the special social and economic requirements of the community which it serves.
>
> Clearly no city government, no citizen agency, no community can achieve efficiency in any branch of city service merely by bringing about precision, orderliness and economics . . . . Ef-

ficient government must match its efforts against a background of knowledge regarding opportunities for service.[38]

Allen once objected to a state law that exempted New York City from filing certain reports while the city was understaffed. His complaint was, "That's as undemocratic as can be. It's against efficiency."[39] Modern commentators might say the law aids efficiency, allowing personnel to concentrate on task fulfillment rather than public communication. For Allen, efficiency is inextricably linked to information exchange.

Like Cooke, Bureau writers consider efficiency valuable only in the service of public desires. Bruere gives an example from school site selection. First, the Board of Education takes community wants into account in deciding how to choose a school site; after that, construction experts report strategies for building the best structure for the fewest dollars. If the school is built in a popular locale, efficient design can only be useful, but Bruere explicitly cautions that "unwise location of school buildings . . . is not mitigated by economy and efficiency in school construction."[40] The goal is not simply building at least cost. It is satisfying the community, one tactic being efficient construction.

In a 1984 *Public Administration Review* article, Robert Goodin and Peter Wilenski contrast what they see as the traditional view, that efficiency is the paramount administrative goal, and their own view, that efficiency is subordinate to want satisfaction, i.e., the only good reason to use resources efficiently is that this satisfies more wants.[41] But such an argument is precisely the one Bruere also constructs. He predates Goodin and Wilenski by many years in viewing efficiency as an instrumental means of achieving political want satisfaction, of use only when it serves the meta-goal of responsiveness.

The zeal for responsiveness in the traditional literature leads at least three BMR writers to take political stands supportive of want satisfaction but diametrically the opposite to what modern authors tell us the municipal reform movement represents. Cleveland, with all his hatred for machines and bosses, nevertheless puts such a high premium on responsiveness that he argues that a boss in touch with public opinion is closer to the scientific management spirit than an elected legislature inadequately apprised of community wants.[42] The reformer's task is to provide forums for elected legislators to learn what bosses already know.

Bruere takes a stand identical with Cooke's in opposing state boards acting as unelected intermediaries between city publics and crucial decisions. Discussing the regulation of public utilities in New York City, he bemoans that,

> In the history of our democracy . . . the regulation of . . . the greatest city in America should be vested in a state commission appointed by the governor and absolutely irresponsible to the community whose interests it is intended to serve.[43]

Although our urban politics textbooks tell us the municipal reformers favored commission structures, Beard faults this form of city government because:

> It destroys the deliberative and representative element in municipal government, and may readily tend to reduce its administration to a mere routine business, based largely upon principles of economy, to the exclusion of civic ideals. Election at large prevents the representation of minorities; and nonpartizan [sic] elections, in addition to being impossible, are based upon the erroneous notion that there can be no real party divisions on municipal politics.[44]

Strange talk indeed for a man who supposedly regards economy as the goal of city administration and prefers an apolitical theory of municipal management.

Modern neglect of the BMR's focus on responsiveness arises partly because contemporary authors are preoccupied with efficiency/responsiveness or efficiency/equity trade-offs.[45] Bureau writers are concerned with the many situations where efficiency is a prerequisite to these other values. When modern writers see the word "efficiency," they do not think of responsiveness. Yet Allen's contemporaries seem to have understood responsiveness as his chief concern even where the word "efficiency" predominates in his work. A 1907 review of his *Efficient Democracy* is not beguiled by the title or chapter headings into neglecting the central concern; the review's author notes that Allen's aim is to relate agency management to citizen knowledge. The title may use "efficient," but the basic interest understood is how to develop information so as to foster responsiveness.[46]

Bureau writers would be stung by most modern summaries of their work but few criticisms would seem as likely to wound them as Terry Cooper's assertion that their using experts to gather information "tended to subvert active citizenship."[47] Close reading of Bureau literature shows that providing the means to make government responsive to such citizenship constituted the *raison d'être* of all their labors.

One can fault Bureau writers for having an amorphous conception of political responsiveness, for not defining the appropriate public to which policy should respond nor the procedures for measuring its will. (Beard is the only BMR writer who explicitly discusses group conflict as an inevitable aspect of city politics.[48]) As Cooke's responsiveness was a vague ideal, so too is the Bureau's, but it is this ideal—and not least-cost efficiency—that the BMR literature offers as the goal of governmental action.

Facts and Paradigms

A third modern criticism of early public administration writers centers on their interest in information. It deplores the types of data they collected, particularly their adherence to the primacy of facts. Again, Waldo seems to have been the first to assert that the BMR's interest in gathering information translates into an assumption that accumulating sufficient facts automatically imparts a sense of direction, eliminating or at least minimizing the role of ideas or paradigms in explaining facts.[49] At various times Bureau writers champion collecting statistics on such topics as: hours spent by public-health nurses caring for patients, demographic characteristics of school leavers, recidivism at different prisons, and cost of electricity per kilowatt hour in various cities. Modern writers could chide their BMR predecessors for not stressing the importance of having a framework for interpreting this type of information when it is available.

Such criticism is rooted in the modern propensity to take facts for granted. We do not need to mount crusades to acquire statistics that are routinely acquired by our governments. BMR writers indicted pre-World-War-I cities for not keeping records or statistics on infant mortality or school-leavers demographic characteristics. While no one, including these BMR writers, assumes records alone will end infant mortality or children's leaving school, few today would argue that having such information would not be useful in understanding such social problems. Now that the data are available, scholars perform a valuable service in showing its limitations, the way demographic statistics do not stand by themselves but need values as a framework for their interpretation. For example, my own article, "Educating Policy Analysts," cautions against facile acceptance of cost/benefit analysis without examining the premises behind the various computations.[50] Before such statistics were kept, scholars performed valuable service in accentuating their significance, that is, their uses in effective democratic policy construction.

The push for facts and more facts does not mean that Bureau writers were blind to the limits of raw data. Reading Allen's work reveals places where he notes the possibility of abusing statistics, but prudently cautions against using this possibility as an excuse not to collect them. He states forthrightly that facts alone do not help people participate in policy making; for this, the public needs facts "presented to disclose their significance," a phrase that seems to imply paradigms and orienting frames.[51] The bulk of Allen's work does not elaborate on this theme; it calls for collecting facts and stresses their potential political uses. But this does not mean that he was unaware of the importance of theoretical framework or of the difficulties and disagreements in interpreting discrete facts. He simply urges recognition of the important role that facts play in understanding and influencing political decisions and the need to disseminate relevant facts to those with policy interests.

Ironically, the Bureau's ultimate success has meant an America inundated with facts. If citizens wish, they can request enough material on almost any major government program to keep them reading many an evening. In this fact-rich environment the burden of public administration scholarship lies in defining what readers have to bring to these reports to understand them. But if the reports and tables did not exist, a primary task would be to produce them. Those who bring meat to a protein-deficient village without elaborating on the dangers of cholesterol should not be assumed to be ignorant of these dangers; they are simply dealing first with the villagers' protein needs, which may, in a given environment, seem paramount. When the Bureau researchers perceived that American citizens were starved for facts, they spent the bulk of their time trying to provide such data; but this alone is not evidence that there was no understanding of the data's limitations.

Workplace Democracy

A fourth criticism is that this literature does not examine potential trade-offs between efficiency and workplace democracy.[52] This charge is simply a repetition of the one leveled against Taylor that, in quest of efficiency, his management experts stifle worker initiative. But the public sector relevance of this critique also includes whether participatory decision making influences civil servants' political and social orientations and behaviors.[53]

Bureau literature posits that scientific management has internal and external consequences for a police or sanitation agency. The introduction of new information on work techniques changes management as surely as it changes political oversight possibilities for citizens. But the paramount focus of the literature is on the political, rather than the managerial, change. Interest centers on how citizens use the data to hold city administrations accountable, not how agency supervisors handle internal information gathering or implementation of improved technologies.

To the extent that Bureau writers discuss internal implementation, they envision a participative process; they were criticized in their own day for encouraging unwarranted subordinate interference. At a 1914 ASME meeting, Bruere spoke on adapting Taylorism to the police, urging that "in place of cunning and cudgels there must be substituted a policy based upon a knowledge of needs, standards of service."[54] Objections followed when he added that individual policemen should be asked to furnish suggestions. Audience members advised that policemen were incapable of planning and cautioned that their participation would lead to dubious results.[55] The engineer audience did not fault Bruere for stifling workers but rather for giving them too much influence.

Current criticism of Taylor and Bruere as increasing authoritarian relations in the workplace of their time needs to deal with the contemporary response to their work at ASME meetings. If police officers were routinely allowed to add their judgment to planning efforts and Bruere sought to end this, why did his audience not recognize this pattern at the 1914 session? Reaction to Bruere's presentation suggests police agencies did not in fact solicit suggestions; the proposal was novel precisely because it was democratic. (The reaction to Taylor's 1895 paper suggests there were similar authoritarian systems in factories.)

Bruere follows Cooke's orientation—and Taylor's clear directive—that scientific management's implementation requires the participation of affected employees. He bases his conviction on the "latent power" of worker knowledge. He chooses to award information rather than hierarchical status the lion's role in agency decision making. Since he explicitly assumes that workers have their own independent sources of knowledge, this cannot be considered a call for authoritarian patterns; in fact, such reasoning calls for disrupting hierarchical relations where entry-level personnel possess superior relevant data. Thus Bruere perceives the call for efficiency as inextricably linked with participative—rather than authoritarian— management.

The four modern criticisms fare poorly when compared with the actual content of Bureau publications. The charge of wholesale borrowing of business techniques confuses acceptance of particular private sector strategies and philosophies with an inability to understand the unique aspects of public service; Bureau writers borrowed private firm techniques because they saw unique uses for them in the political sphere. Bureau use of scientific management is innately political, and geared to uniquely political purposes. Modern charges of an over-emphasis on efficiency as a goal are simply wrong. Bureau writers do not use least cost as a goal but rather as a strategy for reaching political objectives.

The charge that facts were collected without the development of paradigms does have a basis in the Bureau literature. However, it is difficult to tell if the Bureau's focus on collecting data is based on its insufficient awareness of the need for paradigms or on the realization that the need at that particular time was to foster data collection. Some discussion of the difficulties inherent in interpreting data appears in Allen's work.

The consequences of scientific management for internal structures of public agencies receive less attention in Bureau literature than in the works of Taylor or Cooke. To the extent that Bureau writers focus on motivation, they favor democratic leadership and worker participation in planning. Thus, at least three of the four charges are based on misreadings or partial readings of Bureau literature. Young scholars who get their picture of Allen, Bruere, Cleveland, and Beard through modern books and articles can be advised to read Bureau work for themselves and see if their disciplinary grandfathers are not both less naive and more in touch with supposedly modern questions than the post-World-War-II literature asserts.

Passing the Torch: Textbooks and Scientific Management

In 1911 the Bureau organized a Training School for Public Service. The students, mostly mature professionals with doctorates in economics or political science, were lured by the prospect of hands-on experience doing research on government bureaucracies—training with a call to action. Already knowledgeable about constitutional fundamentals and government structure, they plunged into research projects to "learn through doing, but not through doing alone, rather through doing plus observing freshly, critically and optimistically."[56] Training did not eschew class sessions and seminars—Taylor's *Shop Management* and *Principles* were required reading—but the Bureau founders passed on their philosophy and knowledge primarily through project guidance.[57] For the questions that most interested them, the Bureau teachers believed, "You couldn't get answers out of books. . . .That came just from experience."[58]

Had the Training School generated textbooks, their authors almost certainly would have provided a systematic rationale for adapting scientific management to the public sector. But most of the books published by Bureau affiliates sought to educate a mass audience rather than contribute to public administration scholarship per se. Their authors were more concerned with influencing voting habits than with constructing and teaching theories. That their use of "efficiency" or "responsiveness" seems ambiguous today would probably elicit the retort, if any of the founders were still living, that the public has a general idea of what they mean; they would very likely be amazed at modern political scientists' dogged insistance on creating a precise, specialized vocabulary immune from common sense usage.

No general public administration textbook existed until 1926. Training School and university faculties made do with articles, pamphlets, and books dealing with one or another aspect of public management, such as Goodnow's *Municipal Administration*.[59] But Leonard White's *Introduction to the Study of Public Administration* irreversably altered the educational landscape.[60]

This first general textbook offered the field a chance to assess its origins and state of knowledge in a setting restricted to acolytes in the discipline itself. White, a University of Chicago political science professor (1920–1956), had written a 1925 monograph on morale with no mention of Taylor or scientific management.[61] White's textbook, however, gives ample attention to Taylor's contribution, not by analyzing scientific management's impact on morale and motivation (as modern textbooks might do), but rather by focusing on its political ramifications. In an analysis reminiscent of Cooke or the Bureau, White argues that the past one hundred years have seen immense social changes, particularly in technology. These advances suggest new areas where government can make a difference with trained personnel. Scientific management is important because the possibilities inherent in its use make people dissatisfied with traditional agency work systems; a government that does not use its insights will have a dissatisfied citizenry.[62] White's justification for adaptation of scientific management to the public sector echoes the argument for social betterment through responsiveness used by Cooke and Bureau writers. This first public administration textbook incorporates the traditional Progressive/municipal reform views for using Taylor's ideas in the public sector.

Treatment of scientific management is more perfunctory in William F. Willoughby's *Principles of Public Administration*, which appeared in 1927. The author, director of the Washington, D.C., Institute for Government Research, never mentions Taylor but makes the familiar argument that the twentieth-century state is involved in many more activities than its predecessors; administration is more complex, and therefore experimentation is necessary to produce information about its work that will hold public servants accountable to the public's desire for higher standards of efficiency.[63] In truncated form this is the argument underlying adaptation of scientific management to the public sector in the longer, more carefully reasoned accounts by Cooke and the Bureau.

John Pfiffner's 1935 *Public Administration* and 1940 *Research Methods in Public Administration* return to an explicit discussion of Taylor.[64] The University of Southern California professor declared that Taylor had revolutionized business by establishing individual performance standards. Taylor's adapters had created a "new public administration" whose essence is fact finding and research.[65] But Pfiffner argued that Taylor's example called not only for doing research but for using the results as a mechanism for change, both administratively and politically.[66]

Pfiffner is less sanguine than earlier writers about the extent to which Taylor's insights can be transferred to government; in his view, such activities as the administration of justice may be too intangible to support performance standards.[67] This caution can be expected as a reaction against the optimism of public administration's earliest years. Pfiffner's was a noteworthy, and for the time novel, questioning of the scope of scientific management, that is, whether the theory is universally applicable to all government functions. It is not a repudiation of Taylor's importance or the vitality of his ideas; Pfiffner advocates Taylorism's shaping the public administration curriculum.[68] Neither does it repudiate the view of earlier textbooks that Taylor's fundamental gift to public administration was methodological, a call for research with potential use as a mechanism for administrative and political change. Despite certain reservations, Pfiffner's portrait of scientific management is much closer to White's than to the one proferred in modern textbooks.

The Hawthorne Experiments and Early Textbooks

The famous Hawthorne, Illinois, Western Electric production experiments began in the late 1920s, just when the White and the Willoughby textbooks appeared. The three principal works based on the Hawthorne research were published in 1933, 1939, and 1941, respectively.[69] The authors do not let modesty prevent them from making some very striking claims for their research. Without mentioning Taylor nor citing his work, they assert that everyone else working on the motivation problem has defined it in economic terms, disregarding social and human factors.[70] They claim to correct this imbalance by examining the nuances of the Hawthorne factory's social relationships.

Virtually the entire public administration literature of the 1930s ignored this claim. No mention of Hawthorne appears in any major textbooks of the era. White's second (1939) and third (1948) editions give Taylor similar treatment to that extended in the first edition. His work is related to the scope and nature of the discipline rather than to workers' individual motivation. No comparisons are made between scientific management and any alleged human relations approaches. White must have been very well aware that Mayo's claim was excessive; White's own 1925 monograph on morale thoroughly treats noneconomic factors.[71]

To the extent that monographs and collections of articles discuss Mayo's work, it is as an extension of scientific management, simply another example of researchers using work measurements to further industrial cooperation. The most visible pre-war use of the Hawthorne experiments occurs in a chapter in the 1937 book co-edited by Luther Gulick,[72] who, in a sense, inherited Allen, Bruere, Cleveland, and Beard's collective mantle by succeeding the last as director at the BMR Training School in 1921. Gulick's own preface includes no special word of explanation for including an article on the Western Electric experiments; instead, it identifies all the contributions to the volume, including Mayo's, as examples of people thinking scientifically about labor-management cooperation.[73] Instead of presenting Hawthorne as a seminal experiment irretrievably lowering the value of Taylor's contributions, Gulick sees the now-fabled Western Electric work as a relatively minor exercise using insights already formulated by earlier writers.[74] His own piece makes plain that Mayo has no monopoly on concern for nonauthoritarian leadership or noneconomic rewards; he speaks of the dominance of ideas as an alternative to authority structures, a way to get each worker to use skill and enthusiasm "of his own accord."[75]

On the eve of America's entry into World War II, public administration's portrayal of scientific management differs little from the understanding prevalent in 1910 or 1920. Those who quote Taylor or use his insights concentrate on his having showed the discipline that administrative analysis is both possible and important, not as an ivory tower activity valuable in and of itself, but as a change instrument with change emphatically linked to political activities. Taylor's work is seen in a positive light because it holds potential for increasing political responsiveness by maximizing the connection between public management and the attainment of the public's desires. His name is linked with the search for a more democratic democracy.

Chapter 8

Scientific Management and Public Administration: Act Two ─────────

Taylor as villain makes his debut in a 1947 article by Robert Dahl contrasting scientific management with the social, humanistic thrust of the Hawthorne experiments.[1] This article breaks new paths in two directions. It is one of the first to consider Taylor principally as the expositer of a particular motivation system rather than to concentrate on the methodological or political consequences of his work. In a break from public administration tradition, it delineates the negative possibilities inherent in work systematization, condemning Taylor's ideas as narrow, oblivious to personality differences, and overly rational. The motivation system of scientific management is examined and found wanting.

The public administration discipline studies internal and external aspects of agency life and the interactions between them. Internal categories include motivation and control systems while the external aspects of public-agencies involve relations with the entire political system, particularly oversight institutions and the citizenry.

Unlike what students might infer from modern textbooks, prewar writers are intrigued with scientific management primarily because it holds the promise of renewing the democratic nature of city agencies' relations with their constituencies. The appreciation of Taylor assumes that adapting his methodologies to city bureaucracies can increase their responsiveness and accountability.

Beginning with Dahl, the public administration literature assumes that at best Taylor offers discrete techniques for organizing internal motivation and control.[2] Scientific management is no longer presented as a philosophy of hope—a chance for knowledge to redeem a corrupt, unresponsive political system. It is simply a scheme for offering employees certain incentives, and an ineffective scheme at that. Dahl challenges the discipline's understanding of Mayo as well as of Taylor. In his denigration of scientific management, he claims that the work at Hawthorne shattered Taylor's narrow suppositions about human behavior and recognized the true complexity of human purposes and values.

He insists that Mayo's article in *Papers on the Science of Administration* (Gulick's 1937 collection) "properly interpreted, contradicts the implicit assumption of every other essay in that volume."[3] The key phrase is "properly interpreted" by Dahl as editor since Gulick in fact presents the piece as much less revolutionary. For him, it was simply part of a long analytic effort started by others, principally Taylor. For Dahl, it repudiates stifling orthodoxy.

Dahl's interpretation of a proper reading is clear. The one best way of reading Taylor and Mayo is to find Taylor problematic and accept Mayo's estimate of his own importance. Not as clear is how Dahl arrives at this turnabout of traditional interpretations, since he offers no detailed reanalysis of arguments in Taylor's *Shop Management*, *Principles*, or *Testimony*, or the works based on the Hawthorne experiment. He is simply staking a claim—a brave effort under the circumstances—and implicitly inviting other scholars to come up with the evidence. After they do, a new consensus can form around the new Taylor/Mayo divide.

Dwight Waldo and the New Consensus

The supporting evidence appears in Dwight Waldo's *The Administrative State*, a 1942 Yale dissertation revised for publication in 1948.[4] Waldo, who assumes the novel burden of presenting the public administration movement's development as a part of the history of American political thought, does not validate Dahl's perspective by elaborating directly on the Taylor/Mayo dichotomy. Far from glorifying the insights from the Hawthorne experiment, he offers no comparison between Taylor and Mayo's arguments, preferring to follow the practice of earlier scholars and consign the Western Electric experiments to a brief note.

His importance for confirming Dahl's assertion arises from the conceptual linkages he posits between pre-World-War-II public administration and scientific management, linkages that damn the former and the latter both. His argument is that scientific management is the most important influence on the pre-war discipline and that this influence has led the field into at least four nontrivial errors: (1) indiscriminate over-reliance on business concepts, (2) use of efficiency as a goal, (3) acceptance of the primacy of facts, and (4) inattention to workplace democracy. Scientific management has proven an inadequate foundation for understanding public agencies, thus necessitating new, more explicitly political underpinnings. Although almost no mention is made of Hawthorne, a person who found Dahl's article before reading *The Administrative State* might well conclude that more attention to Mayo's work would alleviate the earlier neglect of workplace democracy. One part of the book's strong influence came from its appearance after 1947; Waldo himself has noted that the argument would have looked much stranger had it been published earlier.[5]

Even in 1948, it was an original argument since the bulk of published material gave a very different picture. Arthur Macmahon's review essay in the *Public Administration Review* asserts the prevailing consensus in challenging Waldo's brief that the pre-war literature was apolitical, arguing instead that its sense of purpose emanates from an explicitly political desire to expand the welfare state. Macmahon also disputes the charge that efficiency was used as a goal rather than a strategic servant of democracy.[6]

My own survey of the pre-war works was completed without seeing Macmahon's piece; nevertheless our interpretations of this literature are almost identical. The difference is in tone. He chides Waldo in a few paragraphs as befits a man who restates opinions held by most of his colleagues, I would not at this late date express the same views without extensively quoting pre-war authors. I need to back up such assertions, because they now challenge the consensus of the post-war discipline.

Macmahon's approach was understandable in 1948, but retrograde only two years afterwards. He seems unaware that a new concurrence is forming that takes for granted the inadequacy of the pre-war public administration literature and its scientific management antecedents.

Textbooks convey disciplinary consensus. Their authors decide which ideas are worthy of inclusion in the canon passed on between generations. The evidence of Dahl's triumph comes in 1950 when Herbert Simon co-authors a textbook that, without directly mentioning Taylor, identifies Mayo and Roethlisberger as the first to explore motivation's human factors, implying that economics had preoccupied all previous theorists.[7] As the first major textbook to mention Mayo's work in any context, it can be held responsible for disseminating two new views: (1) Students of public administration have more to learn from the experiments at Hawthorne which are discussed, than Taylor's at Midvale, which are not even mentioned; (2) a dichotomy exists between rigid and authoritarian pre-Hawthorne theories and Mayo and Roethlisberger's work, which recognizes the complexity of human values.

After the appearance of this textbook at the start of the 1950s, a shift occurs in the discipline's consensus about the relative and contrasting usefulness of Taylor and Mayo, with only a few lonely voices standing out against the tide. Perhaps the last in a major publication is management consultant, Merrill Collett, who in a 1962 *Public Administration Review* symposium objects to the emphasis others give Mayo; "I confess to some impatience with what is presented as research but actually represents an attempt to . . . rearrange thoughts previously stated by a different school."[8] By then, this outlook decidedly represents a minority view; most public administration scholars have stopped seeing Hawthorne as a continuation of Taylor's work, preferring to regard the experiments at the Western Electric plant and their interpretation as a counterweight to all that had gone before.

That a shift occurred between 1947 and 1962 is unmistakable. The question is, "Why?" Taylor's work always contained enough contrasting material to spark controversy. Many passages show a commitment to worker development and participation; others, such as the notorious Schmidt narrative, imply a condescending attitude. Those who want to condemn Taylor can find quotations to support their view, but these quotes comprise a miniscule fraction of Taylor's oeuvre. Why did writers before 1947 choose to emphasis the arguments for worker development through participation, while those afterwards leaped at the more authoritarian quotations?

The answer cannot be that post-war writers were more sensitive to slurs against worker intelligence. The Hawthorne works abound with condescending arguments. An us–them attitude prevails throughout. Mayo explicitly champions creating an administrative elite, the charge so often laid at Taylor's door;[9] Roethlisberger refers to motivation as "handling" workers, and once even as "handling Tom, Dick, and Harry."[10]

Management is presented as a clinical activity. Supervisors serve as psychiatrists-without-license, ferreting out the hidden causes of employees' behaviors to obtain "control through an understanding of situations."[11] This leads to a grotesque tendency to psychoanalyze the workers, with no consideration given to the difference between an analyst trying to help patients and a manager grasping at personal information only for the good of the company.

No one suggests that the workers might use their own cunning to psychoanalyze the managers (or the researchers) to achieve their own goals. Ability to understand people is decidedly a one-way street.

A telling difference between Taylor and the Hawthorne experimenters is the attitude of each toward rate cuts. Both Taylor and Roethlisberger encounter workers who will not produce at top speed in a piece-work system. In both cases, the employees believe that pay incentives are a trap so supervisors can learn how quickly a job can be done; armed with this knowledge, management will cut piece rates and raise quotas, compelling workers to work at top speed simply to make the same wages they had formerly earned working at a slower pace. What is Taylor's attitude towards this employee fear? Fury that managers would be so deceptive. Roethlisberger dismisses the worker's concern, calling it irrational because no cuts had yet occurred at the Hawthorne plant.[12] If public administration analysts want a dichotomy in approach, why not present this one?

Very few writers castigate Mayo or Roethlisberger for their lapses. Robert Miewald is one of the few to express repugnance at their attempt to manipulate workers for organizational ends.[13] Most public administration work on this theme presents the psychological manipulation at Hawthorne as an improvement on Taylorism.

Again, the question is "why?", or more explicitly, why set up a shaky Mayo/Taylor contrast without alerting readers that material in both authors defies easy dichotomizing? Why present Taylor's ideas as "authoritarian" without explaining that previous generations of scholars and political activists accepted these same ideas as liberating? (One could offer readers representative quotations supporting each view and allow them to make up their own minds.)

Answering these questions is crucial even to those in public administration with no interest in motivation theory, because the impetus for the modern practice of damning Taylor comes from a misperception many public administration scholars have had about how different key materials in the history of their discipline relate to each other. Using the physical sciences as a model, these scholars assume that works produced at any point in time must have improved on their predecessors, and will, in turn, be superseded by still better and more useful works in time to come. Astronomy moves from Ptolmey to Copernicus to Galileo. Physics progresses from Aristotle's laws of motion to Newton's and then Einstein's. Administrative science starts with a narrow picture of motivation and then improves the usefulness of its paradigm.

Once scholars accept this natural science model of progress as a priori the only valid framework for comparing and evaluating works in an academic discipline, the model itself can easily assume the function of a mold distorting the shape of historical theories. Eager to show that successive schools of thought yield an increasingly refined understanding of nature, believers emphasize aspects of historical works that preserve the assumption of progress even where these aspects are not those parts of their work that the original authors themselves considered crucial.

Analysis of primary sources shows that the picture of a reductionistic Taylor superseded by a more wholistic Mayo distorts historical reality; Taylor and his disciple, Cooke, introduced many ideas for which Mayo and later writers have reaped the credit. The natural science model does not explain the actual relationship between scientific management and its successor theories. Public administration scholars were too quick to suppose that new research would outdistance the old rather than simply repeat concepts in a novel style. Their notion of how thought develops prodded them to encapsulate early theories in a framework that deliberately underplays strengths and inflates weaknesses of the earlier theories in a given field. They need to show Taylor as "primitive" in his thinking to validate the evolutionary model of intellectual development they have adopted.

A more realistic model for relating the earlier to the later public administration literature comes from the arts. The artistic enterprise is based on the historical diversity of equals rather than a notion of linear progress. In music, painting, and poetry, styles succeed one another without necessarily invalidating their predecessors. Dante does not supplant Homer, nor Beethoven, Bach, although the way moderns read Homer or hear Bach is influenced by their reading later literature and their listening to nineteenth- and twentieth-century composers.

Using a model from development in the arts to relate ideas from different historical periods in public administration involves two considerations: (1) giving respect to each work as an entity on its own rather than primarily as part of a historical progression. This does not mean an absence of analysis of a work's place in a temporal continuum but simply that any such analysis should proceed after a thorough examination of the work itself and with respect for the work's idiosyncratic organization and complexities. (2) Introducing concern for the style of a work as well as its content, i.e., assuming that style by itself is a vehicle for conveying intent and meaning.

The difference between a natural science and an arts-based model is profound, with respect to relating works by content and by style. The natural science model assumes the inevitability of progress in content, which vitiates the need to carefully examine early works, while the arts model supports such examination as the only way to understand the predecessors' meanings. As for style, the natural sciences model underplays its importance (except, perhaps, for the elegance in certain equations), while style is a key component of artistic analysis.

If public administration as a discipline had accepted an arts-based model in the late 1940s, Dahl's dichotomy would not have gained adherents. Scholars would have had no a priori reason to welcome evidence of temporal progress; they would not have expected their discipline to produce developmental contrasts such as those alleged from Taylor to Mayo. When a dichotomy was proposed, they would have had their copies of Taylor's *Shop Management* open and seen for themselves the evidence against easy dichotomization. Instead, an arts-based model would have focused attention on a different Taylor/Mayo disparity—that of their styles.

But in the natural science model, these stylistic differences are basically unimportant. The actual public administration literature rarely, if ever, analyzes Mayo's tone and vocabulary. Yet perhaps the arts model is correct, and the tone is essential to the message. If we assume the usefulness of borrowing from the arts, we might attempt a stylistic analysis of Taylor and Mayo, comparing each to dominant public administration writing styles before and after the Second World War. Such an analysis, offered in the next section, shows convergences between Taylor's style and that of earlier writers; it shows similarities between Mayo's style and that of more contemporary authors, including Dahl. A case can be made that these stylistic analogies are part of the message Taylor and Mayo each have sent the public administration community over time, and that they help explain why the early public administration literature was comfortable with Taylor while modern writers favor Mayo.

Styles of Discourse

Because Taylor and the Hawthorne researchers wrote for different audiences, they use widely different literary styles. Taylor was eager to attract a mass audience: Writing for workers, supervisors, managers, and engineers, he uses familiar expressions, spices his work with fictional dialogue and keeps footnotes to a minimum.

The Hawthorne works are basically accessible only to people with college education. Designed for academics and senior managers, they would not be easy to read for people who lacked a background in psychology. Their footnotes refer to European thinkers such as Freud and Durkheim.

Although Taylor takes the idea of using common, everyday language much further than most contemporary authors, his attempt at comprehensibility accords with the style of academic discourse prevalent in much of the pre-World-War-II engineering and social science literature. Cooke designed his work for a lay audience; so did Allen, Bruere, Cleveland, and Beard (in his capacity as a Bureau administrator/researcher). They knew they had to write clearly to spur people to political action. Even the most academically oriented journals—the *American Political Science Review* and the *Political Science Quarterly*—communicated in a style that could be accessible to people without political science training. Almost all authors used common sense language and a minimum of footnotes. The turn-of-the-century public administration scholar's attitude toward jargon emerges clearly from A. Lawrence Lowell's 1913 American Political Science Association presidential address, where he congratulates the discipline on lacking an esoteric vocabulary and insisting instead on writing in a language outsiders can understand. [14]

From the late 1940s on, almost all social and political disciplines turn inward. Public administration, along with the others, accepted the natural science view that jargon has a function in fostering precision in understanding. [15] Articles in public administration remain more readable than those in many other areas of political science, but the dominant style accepts a jargon difficult for a lay person to understand. A high-school-educated supervisor, say, opening a post-World-War-II *Public Administration Review* might not enjoy reading it.

Two administrative literatures came to exist side by side, separate and decidedly unequal. The first consists of popular works written by people with little grounding in administrative theory. These fast-paced books, crammed with narrative and juicy anecdotes, sustain interest by keeping up a flow of bright, witty but relatively shallow ideas. They are generally unable (or lack the interest) to relate specific vignettes or propositions to a theory of administration or politics.

The second, written primarily by academics, transmits specialized knowledge in most cases for discourse between university professors or their students. (By the 1980s, this literature contained myriad fiefdoms each at least partially sealed off from the others. Specialists in one area may be unaware of terms used in others.) The Hawthorne books are similar in style to the books and articles in this literature, while Taylor's works are in an entirely different stylistic universe.

Dahl approaches Mayo or Roethlisberger as a stylistic brother— each might well assume that the other's works have the correct look for an intellectual product. Using this standard, Taylor looks like a popularizer, a throwback to a pre-scientific era when people writing about society did not realize that jargon aided precision.

A recent article on management history highlights this disparity between images when the authors refer to Taylor as an entrepreneur, Mayo as an intellectual.[16] If an intellectual is someone who originates and analyzes ideas, Taylor certainly qualifies. The authors seem to assume that the word means someone who teaches in a university and uses the modern academic writing style—in which case they were correct indeed that only Mayo would qualify.

There is a second way in which the public administration acceptance of the natural science model undermine's Taylor's position. As noted earlier, the model leads scholars to expect early theories to be supplanted by later ones that are more useful, predisposing them to believe that at some point Taylor should be superseded. In addition, the natural science model's encouragement of jargon influences Taylor's contemporary reception by abetting the suspicion that books in common sense language are shallow and imprecise. Given Taylor's letters on the use of language,[17] it is fair to say that he would almost certainly have deplored Mayo's style for shutting out workers and managers from any discourse on their relationships. But modern scholars, as a group, see something very different in the Hawthorne style. For them, the use of esoteric psychological terminologies gives an aura of intellectual capacity that accords with large, complex, realistic ideas, a more profound orientation to life, than that exhibited by that entrepreneur, Frederick Taylor.

Stylistic analysis points out another, even more surprising, disparity. Considering his intended audience, Taylor was a greater democrat than his detractors. The evidence that he wants workers to participate in planning is in his style—he phrases his arguments in terms at least the more skilled among them can understand.

This style has much to recommend it in a world where the vast majority of Americans are cut off from encountering or debating the thought of the most intelligent writers on public organizations. Obviously, this book is not a polemic against academic discourse. Setting out to write on disciplinary interpretation, I assumed my audience would be primarily public administration specialists, and took advantage of the compression and precision that jargon and footnotes allow. But books on subjects that directly interest the vast lay public—supervisor/employee relations or computers in the workplace—lose something if they are closed to consideration and rebuttal by the very people their pronouncements affect.

That the literature itself never considers this disparity indicates to what extent public administration writers ignore the importance of analyzing a work's intended audience. Such examination is besides the point in physics but is very much to the point in a discipline concerned with social relations. When writers seek political or organizational participation, it seems reasonable to inquire whom they expect to participate in debating their proposals. If agency workers are smart enough for administrative decision making, why should language be used to bar them from participating in the academic debate about their role?

The irony is that the pre-war writers whom contemporary articles accuse of favoring expertise over democracy are precisely the professional writers most concerned with opening their discourse to the general public.[18] In the inevitable trade-off between precision and wide comprehensibility, they favor the latter. Rigorous, scientific definitions flourish only after their time. Taylor is quite content to assume that his audience knows what he means by management, even noting, "No concise definition can fully describe an art."[19] (Characteristically, he adds that no matter what its precise, and unobtainable, definition, the relations between employers and workers forms a key component and should be thoroughly studied. He is willing to let approximations carry him as far as they can when partial knowledge is all he has available.)

Stylistic analysis thrusts this irony to the fore by emphasizing that meaning is carried by more than simple denotation. How Taylor or Mayo convey information may be as pertinent to their messages—and their posthumous reputations—as the dictionary or disciplinary meanings of the words each uses. Few public administration students ponder this irony because textbooks afford the only glimpse they get of most historic figures, and such books dissolve stylistic differences among the founders. Admitting that style may be an important variable in evaluating the message offered by early writers, helps highlight the problem of teaching a discipline's history with textbooks, which obliterate all nuances. Where style is important for conveying meaning, textbooks are inappropriate. Only original sources transmit style with content.

Public administration has borrowed the use of textbooks from the natural sciences. Artistic disciplines which recognize stylistic primacy give students ample acquaintance with primary sources. Physics textbooks may preserve the essential historical messages that science students must know, but no one argues that textbooks can convey the full flavor of a Bach sonata. Public administration as a discipline has to confront the question of whether its history is best treated like those of physics or music or to what extent it has to create a deliberate hybrid that recognizes which parts of the natural science model are inappropriate for educating its members. Such a hybrid has to take into account that textbooks have the signal disadvantage of presenting controversies as settled questions while public administration abounds with open controversies. The purpose of our education is not so much to present solutions or even accepted research methods but to unveil longstanding problems (e.g., lack of administrative responsiveness or accountability) for which no accepted solution exists. Questions still appear over how to research or even define key concepts, and early writers may propound insights at least as valuable as their successors'. Such a discipline cannot rely on textbooks to convey the complexities of past thought. Certainly textbooks have been deficient in portraying the complexity of Taylor's thought or that of the municipal reform writers.

Complexity and History

A debate has been in progress since Taylor's heyday on the "real" impact of his work. Neither he nor his modern business-administration defenders (e.g., Louis Fry, Peter Drucker, Edwin Locke) would concede that his denigrators' arguments are persuasive.[20] An open controversy hovers over his work, yet public administration textbooks give no hint that alternative interpretations are possible. Each textbook summarizes scientific management without giving any sense that what is offered is one interpretation. Textbooks never apologize, they never explain, and certainly they never indicate that readers may contest the offered views. This settled attitude may be appropriate for the natural sciences but it is woefully off the mark in public administration.

Distortion is an almost unavoidable result of adopting a natural science model that encourages (1) expecting old theories to serve as foils for the new and (2) teaching through textbooks, making it difficult for students to challenge the accepted view. Dahl titles his 1947 article "The Science of Public Administration: Three Problems." He seems certain that public administration is a science. Taylor seems closer to the mark in using the terms "art" and "science" interchangeably. He recognized that interest in bringing science to management should not preclude a simultaneous interest in creating a management art. While the popular imagination may associate art with sudden, unplanned bursts of imagination, Taylor links composing or painting to careful preparation and the need to learn fundamental principles through long and careful study.[21] He contrasts both art and science with absolute reliance on instinct against which he cautions managers. (He did not consider instinct irrelevant; he simply saw it as insufficient.) He advocates artistic or scientific discipline over hazy instinct; for him the art/science dichotomy is not a question of either/or but rather a taking from both.

Among its characteristics, the discipline of administration possesses some artistic traits, one being that the principal change between early and later contributions can be considered in part stylistic. In public administration, early works often prefigure the content of later writers, with the shift coming in the form of style.

Textbooks are an inappropriate vehicle for conveying these nuances; their use leaves each generation thinking it trumpets new ideals. Look, for example, at the modern movement most concerned with increasing responsiveness—the "new" public administration of the late 1960s and early 1970s.[22] These scholars, with their intense interest in bringing social equity or greater services to the disadvantaged, imagined they offered a novel war cry. Yet their aims often mirror those of an earlier "new" public administration—that associated with the Bureau of Municipal Research. Their essays would have a rounder, more polished orientation if they used the earlier literature to buttress their claims, showing that inadequate government responsiveness is not simply a function of one time or place or their own selective perception but a systemic phenomenon that transcends epochs and many substantive political changes. They cannot do this because all they seem to know of the reform literature is the list of charges against it, the criticisms that make the early writers appear opposed to everything the new iconoclasts long for. The second wave of new public administrators weakens its case by not appreciating that it has sympathetic grandparents.

Public administration students are taught that agency management is difficult; effective action is not always obvious—administrators cannot pretend that all situations have clear solutions. The administrative ambiguities are mirrored in the literature, most of whose key figures cannot easily be pinned down with a single label. Practitioners who posit neat but false dichotomies are heading for disastrous decisions; scholars who set up similar equations lose valuable insights and any sense of their actual history.

Once public administration textbooks propound given views about an individual, writers have an uphill battle changing these perceptions. It may be too late to rescue Frederick Taylor. But with historical perceptions undergirding the core of a discipline's identity, it had better not be too late to rescue public administration from doing an injustice to its progenitors and to its ability to use the past to understand the present.

Chapter 1: Substance and Reputation

1. Daniel Wren and Robert Hay, "Management Historians and Business Historians: Differing Perceptions of Pioneer Contributors," *Academy of Management Journal*, 20 (Sept. 1977), 470–475.

2. Dwight Waldo, *The Administrative State* (New York: Ronald Press, 1948), 209.

3. Works that discuss the social nature of academic disciplines include Barry Barnes, *Interests and the Growth of Knowledge* (London: Routledge and Kegan Paul, 1977), and his *T. S. Kuhn and Social Science* (New York: Columbia University Press, 1982); Stuart Blume, *Towards a Political Sociology of Science* (New York: Free Press, 1974); Robert Merton, *The Sociology of Science: Theoretical and Empirical Investigations*, (Chicago: University of Chicago Press, 1973); Michael Mulkay, *Science and the Sociology of Knowledge* (London: George Allen and Unwin, 1979), and his *The Social Process of Innovation: A Study in the Sociology of Science* (London: Macmillan, 1972); and John Ziman, *Public Knowledge* (London: Cambridge University Press, 1968).

4. Alexander Hamilton, "Federalist No. 11," in *Selections from The Federalist*, Henry Commager, ed. (New York: Appleton-Century-Crofts, 1949), 16.

5. Daniel Sabia, Jr., "Political Education and the History of Political Thought," *American Political Science Review*, 78 (Dec. 1984), 985–999.

6. Sheldon Wolin, "Political Theory as a Vocation," *American Political Science Review*, 63 (Dec. 1969), 1062–1080 (quote on p. 1077).

7. Quentin Skinner, "Meaning and Understanding in the History of Ideas," *History and Theory*, 8 (1969), 3–53 (quote on p. 16).

8. Thomas Kuhn, *The Structure of Scientific Revolutions*, 2nd ed. (Chicago: University of Chicago Press, 1970), 165.

9. Lionel Trilling, *The Experience of Literature* (New York: Holt, Rinehart and Winston, 1969), xi.

10. See Bruno Bettelheim's analysis of the translator's problem in *Freud and Man's Soul* (New York: Knopf, 1983).

11. Chris Argyris, "Some Limits of Rational Man Organizational Theory," *Public Administration Review*, 33 (May/June 1973), 253–267; and Herbert Simon, "Organization Man: Rational or Self-Actualizing?" *Public Administration Review*, 33 (July/Aug. 1973), 346–353.

12. Simon, 346.

13. Skinner, 48–49.

14. For example, see Hans Georg Gadamer, *Truth and Method*, 2nd ed., trans. Garrett Bardin and John Cumming (New York: Seabury, 1975), and Paul Ricoeur, "The Model of the Text: Meaningful Action Considered as a Text," *Social Research*, 38 (1971), 529–562.

15. Charles Wrege and A. Perroni note this habit of inconsistency in "Taylor's Pig-Tale: A Historical Analysis of Frederick W. Taylor's Pig-Iron Experiments," *Academy of Management Journal*, 17 (1974), 6–27. Edwin Locke analyzed Taylor's verbal discrepancies and shows that they do not materially change the argument Taylor makes. See his "The Ideas of Frederick Taylor: An Evaluation," *Academy of Management Review*, 7 (1982), 14–24.

Chapter 2: Taylor in Textbooks

1. Textbooks examined for this project include George Berkley, *The Craft of Public Administration*, 3rd ed. (Boston: Allyn and Bacon, 1981); Marshall Dimock, Gladys Ogden Dimock, and Douglas Fox, *Public Administration*, 5th ed. (New York: Holt, Rinehart and Winston, 1983); George Gordon, *Public Administration in America*, 2nd ed. (New York: St. Martin's Press, 1982); Harold Gortner, *Administration in the Public Sector*, 2nd ed. (New York: Wiley, 1981); Nicholas Henry, *Public Administration and Public Affairs* (Englewood Cliffs, N. J.: Prentice-Hall, 1975); Larry Hill and F. Ted Hebert, *Essentials of Public Administration: A Text with Readings* (North Scituate, Mass.: Duxbury Press, 1979); Jong Jun, *Public Administration: Design and Problem Solving* (New York: Macmillan, 1986); Fred Kramer, *Dynamics of Public Bureaucracy*, 2nd ed. (Cambridge, Mass.: Winthrop, 1981); Carl Lutrin and Allen Settle, *American Public Administration: Concepts and Cases*, 3rd ed. (Englewood Cliffs, N. J.: Prentice-Hall, 1985); Howard McCurdy, *Public Administration: A Synthesis* (Menlo Park, Cal.: Cummings, 1977); Robert Miewald, *Public Administration* (New York: McGraw-Hill, 1973); David Morgan, *Managing Urban America* (North Scituate, Mass: Duxbury Press, 1979); Robert Pursley and Neil Snortland, *Managing Government Organizations: An Introduction to Public Administration* (North Scituate, Mass.: Duxbury Press, 1980); Ira Sharkansky, *Public Administration: Policy-Making in Government Agencies*, 4th ed. (Chicago: Rand-McNally, 1978); Jeffrey Straussman, *Public*

Administration (New York: Holt, Rinehart and Winston, 1985). All but the Dimock book paint unfavorable portraits of Taylor's work. Since the volume by Dimock is a fifth edition, its characterization of scientific management may reflect an earlier more positive approach that I will discuss in Chapter 7. The general tendency of textbooks written in our time is expressed in the other volumes.

2. Henry, 59.

3. Lutrin and Settle, 31.

4. Kramer, 88.

5. Jun, 155.

6. Sharkansky, 199.

7. Jun, 155, and Gordon, 182.

8. Gortner, 199.

9. Berkley, 56–57.

10. Pursley and Snortland, 202.

11. See, for example, the following *Public Administration Review* articles: Albert Guerreiro Ramos, "Models of Man and Administrative Theory" (May/June 1972), 241–246, and "Misplacements of Concepts and Administrative Theory" (Nov./Dec. 1978), 550–557, William Scott and David Hart, "Administrative Crisis: The Neglect of Metaphysical Speculation" (Sept./Oct. 1973), 415–422.

12. Elton Mayo, *The Human Problems of an Industrial Civilization* (New York: Viking, 1933); F. J. Roethlisberger and William Dickson, *Management and the Worker* (Cambridge, Mass.: Harvard University Press, 1939); F. J. Roethlisberger, *Management and Morale* (Cambridge, Mass.: Harvard University Press, 1941).

13. Douglas McGregor, *The Human Side of Enterprise* (New York: McGraw-Hill, 1960).

14. Abraham Maslow, *Motivation and Personality* (New York: Harper and Row, 1954).

15. Sheldon Wolin, *Politics and Vision* (Boston: Little, Brown, 1960), 409.

16. Kenneth Kraemer and John Leslie King show that most public administration scholars writing on computers in organizations predicted that the new technology would have a centralizing influence. As computers made their way into organizations, empirical case studies suggested a more

balanced role for the innovation. "Computing and Public Organizations," *Public Administration Review*, 46 (Nov. 1986), 488–496 (a special issue on public management information systems).

17. Harlan Cleveland, "The Twilight of Hierarchy: Speculations on the Global Information Society," *Public Administration Review*, 45 (Jan./Feb. 1985), 185–195, is a good example of this point of view.

18. See Kraemer and King, and also Kenneth Laudon, *Computers and Bureaucratic Reform* (New York: Wiley, 1974).

19. Frederick Thayer, "Productivity: Taylorism Revisited (Round Three)," *Public Administration Review*, 32 (Nov./Dec. 1972), 833–840 (quote on p. 833).

20. Miewald, 146.

21. Merritt Roe Smith, *Harpers Ferry Armory and the New Technology: The Challenge of Change* (Ithaca, N.Y.: Cornell University Press, 1977), 20.

22. David Noble, *Forces of Production: A Social History of Industrial Automation* (New York: Knopf, 1984), ch. 2.

23. Harley Shaiken, *Work Transformed: Automation and Labor in the Computer Age* (Lexington, Mass.: D.C. Heath, 1986), 18–19.

24. Shaiken, 31.

25. Shaiken, 23.

26. Frederick Thayer, *An End to Hierarchy and Competition*, 2nd ed. (New York: Franklin Watts, 1981); Shaiken, 44.

27. The first quote is from Frederick Taylor, *Shop Management* (1903) (New York: Harper and Row, 1947). The second quote is from Frederick Taylor, *The Principles of Scientific Management* (1911) (New York: Harper and Row, 1947).

28. Sharkansky, 198–199. Sources are Amitai Etzioni, *Modern Organizations* (Englewood Cliffs, N.J.: Prentice-Hall, 1964); James March and Herbert Simon, *Organizations* (New York: Wiley, 1958).

29. Dwight Waldo, *The Administrative State* (New York: Ronald Press, 1948).

30. Robert Dahl, "The Science of Public Administration: Three Problems," *Public Administration Review*, 7 (Winter 1947), 1–11.

31. Ronald Greenwood, Alfred Bolton, and Regina Greenwood, "Hawthorne a Half Century Later: Relay Assembly Participants Remember," in *Readings and Study Guide for Management*, Jane Whitney Gibson, Re-

gina Greenwood, and Ronald Greenwood, eds. (Orlando, Fl.: Academic Press, 1985), 27–35; H. McIlvaine Parsons, "What Caused the Hawthorne Effect? A Scientific Detective Story," *Administration and Society,* 10 (1978), 259–284.

32. Mayo, 172, and Roethlisberger and Dickson, 546–548, make this their own interpretation, a view adopted by the public administration textbooks, sometimes based entirely on secondary sources with no citations of the original Hawthorne research itself (e.g., Sharkansky, 200, or Morgan, 182).

33. Greenwood, Bolton, and Greenwood, 28.

34. Theresa Layman quoted in Greenwood, Bolton, and Greenwood, 28.

35. Peter Drucker, "The Coming Rediscovery of Scientific Management," *Conference Board Record* (June 1976), 23–27.

36. Louis Fry, "The Maligned F. W. Taylor: A Reply to His Many Critics," *Academy of Management Review,* 1 (July 1976), 124–129.

37. Edwin Locke, "The Ideas of Frederick Taylor: An Evaluation," *Academy of Management Review,* 7 (1982), 14–24.

38. The authorized biography is by Frank Copley, *Frederick W. Taylor,* vols. 1–2 (New York: Harper and Bros., 1923). A psychological analysis of some aspects of his life is found in Sudhir Kakar, *Frederick Taylor: A Study in Personality and Innovation* (Cambridge, Mass.: MIT Press, 1970). A concise description of the places Taylor worked and some of his accomplishments appears in Daniel Nelson, *Frederick W. Taylor and the Rise of Scientific Management* (Madison: University of Wisconsin Press, 1980). Unless otherwise noted, material on Taylor's life in later chapters comes from Copley. The appearance of the Kakar and Nelson volumes testifies to contemporary interest in Taylor.

Chapter 3: Early Years

1. Frederick Taylor, personal letter to Morris Cooke, Dec. 2, 1910 in Taylor Collection, Stevens Institute of Technology, Hoboken, N.J.

2. Sudhir Kakar suggests, on the other hand, that Taylor was repudiating his father by not entering the legal profession, an analysis that does not explain why the repudiation involved machine-shop apprenticeship rather than some other non-legal occupation. (See *Frederick Taylor: A Study in Personality and Innovation* (Cambridge, Mass.: MIT Press, 1970), 28–29.)

3. Harley Shaiken, *Work Transformed* (Lexington, Mass.: D. C. Heath, 1986), 16–17.

4. Daniel Nelson, *Managers and Workers: Origins of the New Factory System in the United States, 1880–1920* (Madison: University of Wisconsin Press, 1975), 28.

5. Taylor to Cooke.

6. Frederick Taylor, "Why Manufacturers Dislike College Graduates," *Proceedings of the Society for the Promotion of Engineering Education* (Ithaca, N.Y.: Cornell University, 1909), 79–92.

7. Frederick Taylor, *Testimony before the Special House Committee* (1912) (New York: Harper and Brothers, 1947).

8. Nelson, ch. 3.

9. Henry Metcalfe, *The Cost of Manufactures and the Administration of Workshops Public and Private* (New York: John Wiley and Sons, 1885), 77.

10. Ernest Brown, "The Response of Workers to Scientific Management," in *Scientific Management in American Industry*, Harlow Person, ed. (New York: Harper and Brothers, 1929), 440–447 (quote on p. 440).

11. See, for example, Shaiken's comments on the worker's power in the old system (p. 21).

12. This literature is summarized in Joseph Litterer, "The Emergence of Systematic Management as Indicated by the Literature of Management from 1870 to 1900" (Ph.D. diss., University of Illinois, 1959). Metcalfe's work, along with that of other important figures in systematic management, is discussed later in the chapter. See notes 25, 32, 34, 36, and 37.

13. Nelson, 42.

14. Gerd Korman, *Industrialization, Immigrants and Americanizers* (Madison: Historical Society of Wisconsin, 1967), 63.

15. Harlow Person, "The Origin and Nature of Scientific Management," in Person, 1–22 (quote on p. 2, emphasis in original).

16. U.S. House of Representatives, *Committee to Investigate U.S. Steel Corporation Hearings* (Washington, D.C.; 1912), 2924, quoted in Nelson, 43.

17. "Discussion," *American Society of Mechanical Engineers Transactions*, 12 (1891), 773.

18. See, for example, Foster Rhea Dulles and Melvyn Dubofsky, *Labor in America, A History*, 4th ed. (Arlington Heights, Ill.: Harlan Davidson, 1984), ch. 7.

19. Person, 2.

20. Taylor, *Testimony*, 79–80.

21. Taylor, *Testimony*, 80–84.

22. Taylor, *Testimony*, 85.

23. Taylor, *Testimony*, 83.

24. This seems to be the first time a manager used a time study to determine how people should work; Charles Babbage had previously used it simply to determine how people were actually working. See Daniel Wren, *The Evolution of Management Thought*, 2nd ed. (New York: Wiley, 1979), 125–126.

25. Henry Towne, "The Engineer as an Economist," *American Society of Mechanical Engineers Transactions*, 7 (1886), 428–432.

26. Frank Copley, *Frederick W. Taylor*, vol. 1 (New York: Harper and Brothers, 1923), 434.

27. Paul Van Riper, "Administrative Thought in the 1880s: State of the Art," paper delivered at the American Society for Public Administration Annual Conference, Apr. 1986, 1.

28. Frederick Taylor, *Shop Management* (1903) (New York: Harper and Brothers, 1947), 202.

29. Hugh Aitken, *Taylorism at Watertown Arsenal* (Cambridge, Mass.: Harvard University Press, 1960), ch. 2.

30. Metcalfe, 16.

31. Woodrow Wilson, "The Study of Public Administration," *Political Science Quarterly*, 2 (June 1887), 197–222.

32. Metcalfe, ch. 7.

33. "The American Society of Mechanical Engineers," *Engineering*, 52 (July 3, 1891), 17.

34. Henry Metcalfe, "The Shop Order System of Accounts," *American Society of Mechanical Engineers Transactions*, 7 (1886), 440–448.

35. William Partridge, "Capital's Need for High-Priced Labor," *American Society of Mechanical Engineers Transactions*, 8 (1887), 269–275.

36. Henry Towne, "Gain Sharing," *American Society of Mechanical Engineers Transactions*, 10 (1888), 600–614.

37. Frank Halsey, "Premium Plan of Paying for Labor," *American Society of Mechanical Engineers Transactions*, 12 (1891), 755–764.

38. Quoted in Copley, vol. 1, 400.

39. Frederick Taylor, "A Piece-Rate System Being a Step toward Partial Solution of the Labor Problem," *American Society of Mechanical Engineers Transactions*, 16 (1895), 856–883 (quotes on p. 856).

40. Taylor, "Piece-Rate System," 856.

41. The insight that Taylor predates Maslow in this respect first appears in Louis Fry, "The Maligned F. W. Taylor: A Reply to His Many Critics," *Academy of Management Review*, 1 (July 1976), 124–129.

42. Taylor, "Piece-Rate System."

43. Gustavus Henning, "Discussion," *American Society of Mechanical Engineers Transactions*, 16 (1895), 893–894 (quote on p. 894).

44. William Kent, "Discussion," *American Society of Mechanical Engineers Transactions*, 30 (1908), 1061.

45. Henning.

46. John Hawkins, "Discussion," *American Society of Mechanical Engineers Transactions*, 24 (1903), 1460–1461.

47. "Discussion," *American Society of Mechanical Engineers Transactions*, 24 (1903), 1467.

48. Frank Halsey, "Discussion," *American Society of Mechanical Engineers Transactions*, 16 (1895), 885.

49. Halsey, "Discussion," 886.

50. Copley, vol. 2, 23.

51. Gareth Morgan, *Images of Organizations* (Beverly Hills, Calif.: Sage, 1986), 209.

52. Copley, vol. 1, 388.

53. Taylor, *Shop Management*, 21; for some examples of Taylor's reference to the "art" of management, see pp. 18, 21, 63, 126, or 149, or *The Principles of Scientific Management* (1911) (New York: Harper and Brothers, 1947), 25 or 54.

Chapter 4: Scientific Management

1. For each book, I use the edition published by Harper and Brothers in 1947.

2. Frederick Taylor, "Shop Management," *American Society of Mechanical Engineers Transactions*, 24 (1903), 1337–1456.

3. Frederick Taylor, *Testimony before the Special House Committee* (1912) (New York: Harper and Brothers, 1947).

4. Taylor, *Shop Management*, 21.

5. Taylor, *Shop Management*, 23.

6. Taylor, *Shop Management*, 44.

7. Frank Copley, *Frederick W. Taylor*, vol. 1 (New York: Harper and Brothers, 1923), 234–235.

8. Taylor, *Principles*, 64, 65.

9. Taylor, *Shop Management*, 48.

10. Taylor, *Principles*, 46.

11. Taylor, *Principles*, 60.

12. Taylor, *Principles*, 40, 59.

13. See, for example, his letters to Morris Cooke, Oct. 6, 1910, and to C. Bertrand Thompson of the Harvard Graduate Business School, Dec. 30, 1914 (Taylor Collection).

14. Taylor, *Principles*, 64.

15. Taylor, *Shop Management*, 176–177.

16. Taylor, *Shop Management*, 94–148.

17. Taylor, *Shop Management*, 100–101.

18. Taylor, *Shop Management*, 101.

19. Taylor, *Shop Management*, 28.

20. Frederick Taylor, "Discussion," *American Society of Mechanical Engineers Transactions*, 34 (1912), 1195.

21. Taylor, *Shop Management*, 133.

22. Taylor, *Shop Management*, 60.

23. Taylor, *Principles*, 131; see also Taylor, *Shop Management*, 130.

24. Taylor, *Shop Management*, 130.

25. Taylor, *Principles*, 131–132.

26. Taylor, *Principles*, 9.

27. Taylor, *Principles*, 12.

28. Taylor, *Principles*, 12, and *Shop Management*, 25–26 (quotation p. 26). Wage raises must be permanent to counteract worker fears of the prevailing practice of piece-rate wage cuts once individual output had risen.

29. The need for feedback is already suggested in Taylor's 1895 ASME presentation discussed in Chap. 3.

30. Taylor, *Shop Management*, 184.

31. Taylor, *Shop Management*, 185.

32. Taylor, *Principles*, 34.

33. Taylor, *Principles*, 96.

34. Taylor, *Shop Management*, 133.

35. Frederick Taylor, "The Conservation of Human Effort," paper presented at the City Club of Philadelphia, Jan. 8, 1911 (Taylor Collection).

36. Taylor, *Principles*, 126.

37. Taylor, *Principles*, 126 (italics in original).

38. Taylor, *Principles*, 126–127.

39. The undated letter is from Judge Charles Heydon to Taylor's friend, Birge Harrison. Taylor sends a copy with a letter of his own to Morris Cooke, Sept. 2, 1914 (Taylor Collection).

40. For example, see the discussion in Samuel Yeager, Jack Rabin, and Thomas Vocino, "Feedback and Administrative Behavior in the Public Sector," *Public Administration Review*, 45 (Sept./Oct. 1985), 570–575.

41. Larry Preston, "Freedom and Bureaucracy," *American Journal of Political Science*, 31 (Nov. 1987), 773–795 (quote on p. 781).

42. Taylor, *Principles*, 103.

43. Taylor, *Principles*, 128.

44. Taylor's letter to Morris Cooke, May 5, 1910, gives an example of an employee who was "third-class" at so many jobs that people were "delighted" when he at last proved "first-class" at another task (Taylor Collection).

45. Taylor, *Shop Management*, 28.

46. Quote is from Taylor's *Principles*, 127, but see also his *Shop Management*, 146.

47. Taylor, *Principles*, 127.

48. Taylor, *Shop Management*, 146.

49. Taylor, *Principles*, 127.

50. See Gerald Caiden, "In Search of an Apolitical Science of American Public Administration," in *Politics and Administration: Woodrow Wilson and American Public Administration*, Jack Rabin and James Bowman, eds. (New York: Marcel Dekker, 1984), 51–76 (quote on p. 60).

51. Taylor, *Shop Management*, 140–141.

52. Frederick Taylor to Edwin Gay, Oct. 9, 1913 (Taylor Collection).

53. See the discussion in Henry Gantt, "Training Workmen in Habits of Industry and Cooperation," *American Society of Mechanical Engineers Transactions*, 30 (1908), 1037–1048.

54. Taylor, *Principles*, 130.

55. Taylor, *Principles*, 134.

Chapter 5: Immediate Reception

1. Frederick Taylor to Morris Cooke, Dec. 10, 1910 (Taylor Collection).

2. Frederick Taylor to Morris Cooke, Mar. 29, 1910 (Taylor Collection).

3. Morris Cooke to Frederick Taylor, Mar. 18, 1911 (Taylor Collection).

4. Frederick Taylor to Morris Cooke, Mar. 23, 1911 (Taylor Collection).

5. Morris Cooke to Frederick Taylor, Dec. 10, 1910 (Taylor Collection).

6. He sent the ASME copies out before the serialization appeared, since the Association's Code of Ethics forbade members to discuss professional issues with the public before bringing them to a professional audience.

7. Milton Nadworny, *Scientific Management and the Unions,1900–1932* (Cambridge, Mass.: Harvard University Press, 1955), 39. Sub-Committee on Administration, "The Present State of the Art of Industrial Management," *American Society of Mechanical Engineers Transactions*, 34 (1912), 1140–1147.

8. See Magali Serfati Larson's analysis in *The Rise of Professionalism* (Berkeley and Los Angeles: University of California Press, 1977), 141.

9. For a discussion of Progressivism that emphasizes its role in fostering change, see Richard Hofstadter, *The Age of Reform: From Bryan to FDR* (New York: Alfred Knopf, 1959), and Lawrence Herson, *The Politics of Ideas: Political Theory and American Public Policy* (Homewood: Ill.: Dorsey, 1984), ch. 10. For a discussion of Progressivism as a fundamentally conservative movement useful to large corporations, see Gabriel Kolko, *The Triumph of Conservatism* (New York: Free Press, 1963), and Martin Sklar, "Woodrow Wilson and the Political Economy of Modern U.S. Liberalism," in *For a New America: Essays in History and Politics from Studies on the Left, 1959–1967*, James Weinstein and David Eakins, eds. (New York: Random House, 1970), 46–100.

10. A. Church, "Discussion," *American Society of Mechanical Engineers Transactions*, 34 (1912), 1158.

11. Ida Tarbell, "The Golden Rule in Business," *American Magazine* (Nov. 1914), 11–17; "The Golden Rule in Business: Making the Hire Worthy of the Laborer," *American Magazine* (Feb. 1915), 25–29 and 66; "The Golden Rule in Business: His Own Worst Enemy," *American Magazine* (May 1915), 20–23, 94, 98.

12. Cooke to Taylor, Dec. 10, 1910.

13. Taylor to Cooke, Dec. 10, 1910.

14. See letters and papers in Cooke Collection, Box 168. The Cooke Collection is in the Franklin D. Roosevelt Presidential Library, Hyde Park, New York.

15. Copley, vol. 1, 387.

16. See Alpheus Mason, *Brandeis: A Free Man's Life* (New York: Viking, 1946), ch. 20.

17. See *Evidence Taken by the Interstate Commerce Commission in the Matter of Proposed Advances in Freight Rates by Carriers*, U.S. Senate Document 725, 61st Congress, 3rd sess. (Washington, D.C.: U.S. Government Printing Office, 1911).

18. Frederick Taylor to Louis Brandeis, n.d., but probably late Oct. or very early Nov. 1910, since it responds to Brandeis letter of Oct. 26, 1910 (Taylor Collection).

19. See discussion in Edwin Layton, Jr., *The Revolt of the Engineers: Social Responsibility and the American Engineering Profession* (Cleveland, Ohio: Case Western Reserve University Press, 1971), 156.

20. *Evidence*, vol. 4, 2674–2799 (quote on pp. 2798–2799).

21. See discussion in Cooke's letter to Taylor, Nov. 10, 1910, and Taylor's letter to Brandeis, Apr. 15, 1911 (Taylor Collection).

22. Louis Brandeis, *Business—A Profession* (Boston: Small, Maynard, 1914), p. 3.

23. Brandeis, 41.

24. Louis Brandeis, "Foreword," in Frank Gilbreth's, *Primer of Scientific Management* (1914) (Easton, Penn.: Hive Publishing, 1973), p. vii.

25. Louis Brandeis, "Address," in *Frederick Winslow Taylor: A Memorial Volume* (New York: Taylor Society, 1920), 72–76 (quotes on p. 72).

26. William Kent, "Discussion," *American Society of Mechanical Engineers Transactions*, 30 (1908), 1061.

27. Taylor, *Shop Management*, 94.

28. See Nadworny.

29. Frank Hudson, "The Machinist's Side of Taylorism," *American Machinist* (Apr. 27, 1911), 773.

30. International Association of Machinists, *Official Circular* no. 12, Apr. 26, 1911 (Taylor Collection).

31. Taylor to Thompson, Dec. 30, 1914.

32. Taylor, *Shop Management*, 186.

33. Taylor, *Principles*, 142–143 (quote on p. 143).

34. "Union Hears of Brandeis Idea," *Boston Herald*, Apr. 3, 1911 (Taylor Collection).

35. Taylor, *Shop Management*, 146.

36. Taylor, *Shop Management*, 146.

37. Robert Hoxie, *Scientific Management and Labor* (1915) (New York: Augustus Kelly, 1966).

38. See notes 29 and 30.

39. Morris Cooke to Frederick Taylor, Dec. 22, 1911 (Taylor Collection).

40. Henry Gantt, "Discussion," *American Society of Mechanical Engineers Transactions*, 34 (1912), 1165.

41. Frederick Taylor to Morris Cooke, Jan. 13, 1910 (Taylor Collection). Van Alstyne was a Vice-President of American Locomotive Company; Harrington Emerson was a consultant engineer.

42. Frederick Taylor to H. J. Porter, an industrial engineer who had asked him to join the National Society for Promoting Efficiency, Nov. 6, 1911 (Taylor Collection).

43. Frederick Taylor to E. C. Wolf, editor of the *Ladies Home Journal*, Mar. 11, 1915 (Taylor Collection).

44. Frederick Taylor to Morris Cooke, Jan. 22, 1909 (Taylor Collection).

45. See note 30.

46. Hugh Aitken, *Taylorism at Watertown Arsenal* (Cambridge, Mass.: Harvard University Press, 1960), 212–213.

47. James Mackaen's presentation to U.S. House of Representatives Special Committee to Investigate the Taylor and Other Systems of Shop

Management, *Hearings* (Washington, D.C.: U.S. Government Printing Office, 1912), vol. 1, 339.

48. Aitken (pp. 181–182) argues that the existence of a planning room for the machine shop and not the foundry may be one reason the molders went on strike but the machinists did not.

49. Aitken, 111.

50. U.S. House of Representatives Special Committee, 367–370.

51. U.S. House of Representatives Special Committee, vol. 3, 1923–1924, and Aitken, ch. 4; Orrin Cheney, a machinist, testified on the Major's reaction. U.S. House of Representatives Special Committee, vol. 1, 23.

52. Gen. William Crozier's testimony, U.S. House of Representatives Special Committee, vol. 2, 1165.

53. Frederick Taylor to General William Crozier, June 9, 1911 (Taylor Collection).

54. Carl Barth to Frederick Taylor, Aug. 12, 1911 (Taylor Collection).

55. See Henry Gantt's scathing testimony on this point in U.S. House of Representatives Special Committee, vol. 1, p. 579.

56. U.S. House of Representatives Labor Committee, *Hearings before the Committee on Labor*, 62nd Congress, 1st sess., House Resolution 30 (Washington, D.C.: U.S. Government Printing Office, 1911).

57. Frederick Taylor to Morris Cooke, Aug. 20, 1911 (Taylor Collection).

58. Frederick Taylor to General William Crozier, Sept. 21, 1911 (Taylor Collection).

59. Barth to Taylor, Aug. 12, 1911.

60. Miner Chipman, "Efficiency, Scientific Management and Organized Labor," paper presented at a meeting of the Efficiency Society, Jan. 21, 1916, 13 (Taylor Collection).

61. Aitken, 141.

62. See the statements of James O'Connell, International Association of Machinists president, in U.S. House of Representatives Labor Committee, 34–38.

63. Louis Brandeis to Frederick Taylor, Sept. 14, 1911 (Taylor Collection).

64. A particularly vivid clash took place between Taylor and a Rock Island Arsenal worker, Frank Leonard, who finally admitted, "We seem to be misinformed." U.S. House of Representatives Special Committee, 927–930 (quote on p. 931).

65. The seminal work introducing this notion is Dwight Waldo, *The Administrative State* (New York: Ronald Press, 1948), 202.

66. Taylor, *Testimony*, 26.

67. Taylor, *Testimony*, 30.

68. Taylor, *Testimony*, 29–30.

69. Taylor, *Testimony*, 34.

70. Taylor, *Testimony*, 27.

71. Taylor, *Testimony*, 52–53.

72. Taylor, *Testimony*, 199.

73. Taylor, *Testimony*, 200.

74. U.S. House of Representatives Labor Committee, *Hearings on a Bill to Prevent the Use of the Stop Watch*, 63d Congress, 2nd sess. (Washington, D.C.: U.S. Government Printing Office, 1914), 82.

75. Taylor, *Testimony*, 145.

76. Taylor, *Testimony*, 138.

77. Sub-Committee on Administration, 1146.

78. U.S. House of Representatives Labor Committee, *Hearings to Prevent the Stop Watch*, 3.

79. Aitken, 233.

80. John Greenleaf Whittier, "The Saddest Words" in *The New Pocket Anthology of American Verse*, Oscar Williams, ed. (New York: Washington Square Press, 1961), 593.

81. Taylor, *Testimony*, 285–286.

82. Daniel Wren, *The Evolution of Management Thought*, 2nd ed. (New York: Wiley, 1979), 143.

83. Taylor, *Testimony*, 153.

84. See, for example his letter to Morris Cooke, July 23, 1909, in which he discusses a job-related imbroglio between Cooke and Gantt (Taylor Collection).

85. Chipman, 2.

86. Thomas Schelling, *The Strategy of Conflict* (Cambridge, Mass.: Harvard University Press, 1960).

87. Chipman, 11.

88. Hoxie, 114.

89. Taylor, *Testimony*, 280.

90. Harlow Person, "Report of the Managing Director: A Decade of Progress," unpublished Taylor Society paper, Feb. 5, 1926 (Cooke Collection).

Chapter 6: Morris Cooke

1. Thomas Haskell, *The Emergence of Professional Social Science: The American Social Science Association and the Nineteenth-Century Crisis of Authority* (Urbana: University of Illinois Press, 1977).

2. See Albert Somit and Joseph Tanenhaus, *The Development of American Political Science* (Boston: Allyn and Bacon, 1967), and David Ricci, *The Tragedy of Political Science: Politics, Scholarship and Democracy* (New Haven, Conn.: Yale University Press, 1984).

3. Somit and Tanenhaus, 55.

4. Joseph Goldberg and William Moye, *The First Hundred Years of the Bureau of Labor Statistics* (Washington, D.C.: U.S. Department of Labor, 1984).

5. Frank Goodnow, *Politics and Administration* (New York: Russell and Russell, 1900).

6. Goodnow, 24–25.

7. *Economic Studies*, vol. 1 (Apr. 1896).

8. Edgar O'Daniel, "Review of Frederick Taylor's *Principles of Scientific Management*," *Political Science Quarterly*, 3 (1912), 534–536.

9. Clyde King to Frederick Taylor, Feb. 21, 1912 (Taylor Collection).

10. J. Russell Smith to Frederick Taylor, Jan. 27, 1915; Frederick Taylor to J. Russell Smith, Feb. 8, 1915 (Taylor Collection).

11. Frederick Taylor to General William Crozier, June 26, 1911 (Taylor Collection).

12. Frederick Taylor, "Government Efficiency," unpublished manuscript (Taylor Collection).

13. A sketch of Cooke's life appears in Kenneth Trombley, *The Life and Times of a Happy Liberal: A Biography of Morris Llewellyn Cooke* (New York: Harper and Brothers, 1954).

14. Charles Merriam and Harold Lasswell, "Current Public Opinion and the Public Service Commission," in *Public Utility Regulation*, Morris Cooke, ed. (New York: Ronald Press, 1924).

15. Charles Wrege and A. Stotka, "Cooke Creates a Classic: The Story behind F. W. Taylor's Principles of Scientific Management," *Academy of Management Review*, 3 (Oct. 1978), 736–749, argue that Cooke actually wrote chapters of Taylor's book and should have been given co-author credit, but that the older and more famous man took the glory for himself. This seems unlikely because Cooke explicitly notes in an unpublished preface that he had only edited the material and did not want "to claim part in a work which had been practically completed before I became associated with it." See Morris Cooke, "Preface," undated manuscript (Taylor Collection).
Wrege and Stotka suggest that Cooke had a less rambunctious personality than Taylor and hence was easily led to forego due acknowledgment. Cooke's political career (particularly his utilities battles of 1915–1917), recounted later in this chapter, belies an acquiescent fellow letting himself be cheated of what he considered rightfully his.

16. Frederick Taylor to Morris Cooke, Nov. 27, 1911, 2, 3 (Taylor Collection).

17. Morris Cooke to Frederick Taylor, Feb. 5, 1910 (Taylor Collection).

18. This correspondence is in the Cooke Collection. In general, the best source for Cooke's pre-1915 letters on scientific management is the Taylor Collection; the Cooke Collection is better for later unpublished materials.

19. Morris Cooke to Louise Taylor, Mar. 28, 1934 (Cooke Collection).

20. Morris Cooke, *Our Cities Awake* (New York: Doubleday, Page and Co., 1918), 86.

21. The charge seems to originate in Dwight Waldo, *The Administrative State* (New York: Ronald Press, 1948). See also Jameson Doig, " 'If I See a Murderous Fellow Sharpening a Knife Cleverly . . . ': The Wilsonian Dichotomy and the Public Authority Tradition," *Public Administration Review*, 43 (July/Aug. 1983), 292–304, and David Rosenbloom, "Public Administrative Theory and the Separation of Powers," *Public Administration Review*, 43 (May/June 1983), 219–226.
But see new research that shows Woodrow Wilson's article was not heavily cited in the formative literature. Daniel Martin, "The Fading Legacy of Woodrow Wilson," *Public Administration Review*, 48 (Mar./Apr. 1988), 631–636.

22. Robert Goodin and Peter Wilenski, "Beyond Efficiency: The Logical Underpinnings of Administrative Principles," *Public Administration Review* (Nov./Dec. 1984), 512–517 (quote on p. 512).

23. Henry Metcalfe, *The Cost of Manufactures and the Administration of Workshops Public and Private* (New York: John Wiley and Sons, 1885), ch. 7.

24. In books such as *Our Cities Awake* Cooke is concerned with applied public management rather than grand theory; he never generalizes to the level of discussing politics in terms of conversion mechanisms in the manner of David Easton, *A Framework for Political Analysis* (Englewood Cliffs, New Jersey: Prentice-Hall, 1965). But his analysis of city politics stresses at the case level the impact of demands and supports and the role of authoritative government as a conversion agent. Cooke would have appreciated Easton's model.

25. Cooke, *Our Cities Awake*, 43, 306.

26. Cooke, *Our Cities Awake*, 267.

27. Waldo, 202. Emphasis in the original.

28. Cooke, *Our Cities Awake*, 74.

29. Morris Cooke, "Some Factors in Municipal Engineering," *American Society of Mechanical Engineers Transactions*, 36 (1914), 605–618.

30. Cooke, *Our Cities Awake*, 167.

31. Albert Smith Faught to Morris Cooke, Mar. 4, 1920 (Cooke Collection).

32. Eliot Bolger (Secretary, Philadelphia Civil Service Commission) to Morris Cooke, Apr. 30, 1913 (Taylor Collection).

33. Frederick Taylor, *Shop Management* (1903) (New York: Harper and Brothers, 1947), 140.

34. Cooke, *Our Cities Awake*, pictures opposite p. 104, and "Some Factors in Municipal Engineering." Contrast these with political scientist A. Lawrence Lowell who in writing about standardizing relatively "low-level" government work refers to postmasters, custom officers, and city finance administrators. *Public Opinion and Popular Government* (New York: Longmans, Green and Company, 1913), 274.

35. See the assessment on New York Mayor John Lindsay in Howard McCurdy, *Public Administration: A Synthesis* (Menlo Park, Calif.: Cummings Publishing Co., 1977), 196.

36. Morris Cooke, "Who Is Boss in Your Shop?" *Annals*, 71 (May 1917), 167–185. See a contemporary assessment in J. A. Dunaway, "Standardization and Inspection," *American Political Science Review* 10 (May 1916), 315–319.

37. For example, Gerald Caiden, "In Search of an Apolitical Science of American Public Administration," in *Politics and Administration: Woodrow Wilson and American Public Administration*, Jack Rabin and James Bowman, eds. (New York: Marcel Dekker, 1984), 51–76.

38. Cooke, *Our Cities Awake*, 98.

39. Cooke, "Some Factors" and *Our Cities Awake*, 97–98.

40. Cooke, *Our Cities Awake*, 97.

41. For the argument that this is what early public administration writers believed, see Herbert Kaufman, "Emerging Conflicts in the Doctrines of Public Administration," *American Political Science Review*, 50 (Dec. 1956), 1057–1073. Kaufman asserts that early writers favored independent boards to separate politics and administration. Cooke flatly opposes using boards as intermediaries between elected officials and the public. Since in his understanding, efficiency should be used only in the service of responsiveness, these boards are labelled a bar to efficiency! *Our Cities Awake*, 66.

42. Morris Cooke, *How about It?* (Lancaster, Penn.: New Era Printing Co., 1917).

43. Michael Harmon and Richard Mayer, *Organization Theory for Public Administrators* (Boston: Little, Brown, 1986), 98.

44. Cooke, "Some Factors," 613.

45. Morris Cooke, "The Spirit and Social Significance of Scientific Management," paper delivered at the Western Economic Association Annual Meeting, Chicago, Mar. 14, 1913, 12 (Taylor Collection).

46. Harmon and Mayer, 98–102.

47. Cooke, "Spirit and Significance," 12.

48. Frederick Taylor to Louis Brandeis, n.d. (but almost certainly late Oct./early Nov. 1910), 4–5 (Taylor Collection). Taylor showed Cooke a copy of the letter while Cooke was helping Brandeis prepare the railroad freight tarriff case.

49. Douglas McGregor, *The Human Side of Enterprise* (New York: McGraw-Hill, 1960).

50. Abraham Maslow, *The Further Reaches of Human Nature* (New York: Viking, 1971), 43.

51. Cooke, "Who Is Boss?"

52. Cooke, *Our Cities Awake*, 98.

53. Cooke, "Who Is Boss?" 178.

54. Taylor, *Shop Management*, 25.

55. Chester I. Barnard, *The Functions of the Executive* (Cambridge, Mass.: Harvard University Press, 1938), 165.

56. Cooke, "Who Is Boss?" 182.

57. Morris Cooke, "Public Engineering and Human Progress," paper presented to the Cleveland Engineering Society, Nov. 14, 1916, 8 (New York Public Library).

58. Morris Cooke, *Snapping Cords: Comments on the Changing Attitudes of American Cities* (privately printed, 1915), 24.

59. Morris Cooke to Louis Brandeis, Oct. 15, 1914 (Taylor Collection).

60. Morris Cooke to Mayor Rudolph Blankenburg, Jan. 30, 1913 (Taylor Collection). This letter lays out the whole incident for future legal action. A copy was sent to Taylor.

61. Cooke, *Snapping Cords*, 1.

62. Cooke to Brandeis, Oct. 15, 1914.

63. "Public Policies to Municipal Utilities," program of conference, Nov. 12–14, 1914 (Taylor Collection).

64. Morris Cooke to Frederick Taylor, July 23, 1914 (Taylor Collection).

65. Morris Cooke to Frederick Taylor, Sept. 23, 1914 (Taylor Collection). The Board eventually included Brandeis; Taylor; Frederick Cleveland, New York Bureau of Municipal Research; Samuel Fels, manufacturer; Felix Frankfurter, Harvard Law School (a Brandeis protege); Charles Jenkins, publisher of the *Farm Journal*; Leo Rowe, professor of political science at the University of Pennsylvania; and Charles Van Hise, president of the University of Wisconsin. For the Brandeis influence in Frankfurter's selection, see Morris Cooke, letter to Louis Brandeis, July 9, 1914, and Louis Brandeis, letter to Morris Cooke, July 10, 1914 (Taylor Collection).

66. Cooke to Brandeis, Oct. 15, 1914.

67. Cooke to Blankenburg, Jan. 30, 1913, and to Samuel Bodine (President, United Gas Improvement Company), Feb. 28, 1913 (Taylor Collection).

68. Cooke, *Snapping Cords*, 12. In 1922, Cooke argued that the National Electric Light Association should not be allowed to be a tenant in the Engineering Societies Building because it refused to share its information with the public. Morris Cooke to Robert Wolf (a scientific management advocate), May 25, 1922 (Cooke Collection).

69. The lectures are published in *Snapping Cords*. The engineers were M. E. Cooley, Dean of Engineering, University of Michigan; Alexander Humphreys, President, Stevens Institute of Technology; Dugald Jackson, Professor of Electrical Engineering, Massachusetts Institute of Technology; and George Swain, Professor of Civil Engineering, Harvard University.

70. Cooke, *How about It?*, 35.

71. Morris Cooke to C. W. Baker, Jan. 3, 1916, reprinted in *How about It?*, 34.

72. Morris Cooke to Calvin Rice, March 7, 1916, reprinted in *How about It?*, 34.

73. Letters in Cooke Collection, Box 168.

74. Calvin Rice (Secretary of ASME Council) memo to Council Members, Mar. 3, 1915 (Cooke Collection).

75. Cooke, *How about It?*, 17.

76. Morris Cooke to C. W. Baker, June 4, 1915, reprinted in *How about It?*, 45.

77. Morris Cooke to William Chantland (Attorney, Federal Trade Commission), Sept. 13, 1928 (Cooke Collection).

Chapter 7: Scientific Management and Public Administration: Act One

1. Avery Leiserson, "The Study of Public Administration," in *Elements of Public Administration*, Fritz Morstein Marx, ed. (Englewood Cliffs, N. J.: Prentice-Hall, 1946), 27–50. See also Alice Stone and Donald Stone, "Early Development of Education in Public Administration," in *American Public Administration: Past, Present, Future*, Frederick Mosher, ed. (University: University of Alabama Press, 1975), pp. 11–48.

2. Charles Goodsell, "Charles A. Beard, Prophet for Public Administration," *Public Administration Review*, 46 (Mar./Apr. 1986), 105–107 (quote on p. 106).

3. A history of the Bureau appears in Jane Dahlberg, *The New York Bureau of Municipal Research* (New York: New York University Press, 1966). Allen's attitude towards his financial benefactors seems ambiguous. The BMR criticized Rockefeller and Carnegie but Allen's 1949 reminiscences contain what can only be called name dropping, perhaps to show that he could enlist the support of rich, prominent people. See William Allen, "Reminiscences," Dec. 1949–Feb. 1950, unpublished manuscript in Columbia University's Oral History Collection.

4. Allen, vol. 1, 99–100.

5. See Charles A. Beard, "Philosophy, Science and Art of Public Administration," address to the Governmental Research Association, Princeton, N. J., Sept. 8, 1939, 1 (New York Public Library).

6. Charles A. Beard, *An Economic Interpretation of the Constitution of the United States* (New York: Macmillan, 1913). Analysis of Beard's work as an historian appears in Richard Hofstadter, *The Progressive Historians* (New York: Knopf, 1968).

7. See Frederick Cleveland, "The Application of Scientific Management to the Activities of the State," address at Dartmouth College, Oct. 18, 1912; available at the Institute of Public Administration, New York City.

8. Cleveland was one of the early choices. See Morris Cooke to Louis Brandeis, July 9, 1914 (Taylor Collection).

9. See, for example, Morris Cooke's letters to Frederick Cleveland, Nov. 5, 1926, and Sept. 6, 1921, and Cleveland's letter to Cooke, Sept. 29, 1922 (Cooke Collection).

10. Charles Burlingham, "Introduction," David Snedden and William Allen, *School Reports and School Efficiency* (New York: Macmillan, 1908), 1.

11. Allen, vol. 1, 159. The same thought in slightly different form appears in *Snedden and Allen*, 8, and Frederick Cleveland, *Organized Democracy* (New York: Longmans, Green and Company, 1913), 454 and in other publications by Bureau writers.

12. Bureau of City Betterment of the Citizens Union of New York, *The Police Problem in New York City* (New York: Citizens Union, 1906), 1–12. This report was drafted by Henry Bruere for the Bureau of City Betterment.

13. We may now be in the midst of such a shift. See, for example, the articles in the mini-symposium on "Privatization: Limits and Applications," *Public Administration Review*, 47 (Nov./Dec. 1987), 453–484.

14. This line of thought appears in most Bureau writings, including William Allen, *Efficient Democracy* (New York: Dodd, Mead and Co., 1907). It is most explicitly and emphatically treated in Frederick Cleveland, "Municipal Ownership as a Form of Governmental Control," *Annals*, 35 (1906), 359–370, and in Frederick Cleveland with the assistance of Clarence Smith, *Principles of Government Organization and Management* (Washington, D.C.: Army Education Commission, 1919), 89.

15. Cleveland, *Principles*, 102.

16. Henry Bruere, *The New City Government* (New York: D. Appleton and Co., 1912), 13.

17. Cleveland, *Principles*, 89.

18. *Report of Reconstruction Commission to Governor Alfred E. Smith on Retrenchment and Reorganization in the State Government*, Oct. 10, 1919, 4–5, quoted in Luther Gulick, "Beard and Municipal Reform," in *Charles Beard*, Howard Beale, ed. (Lexington: University of Kentucky Press, 1954), 47–60. Beard drafted the Reconstruction Commission's report.

19. For example, Snedden and Allen, 2, and William Allen, "Instruction in Public Business," *Political Science Quarterly*, 22 (1908), 604–616.

20. Dahlberg, 12.

21. George Graham, *Education for Public Administration* (Chicago: Public Administration Service, 1941), 140–141.

22. Charles A. Beard, *American City Government* (New York: Century Company, 1912), 79.

23. First articulated in Dwight Waldo, *The Administrative State* (New York: Ronald Press, 1948).

24. Quoted in Graham Allison, Jr., "Public and Private Management: Are They Fundamentally Alike in All Unimportant Respects?", in *Current Issues in Public Administration*, Frederick Lane, ed., 2nd edition (New York: St. Martin's Press, 1982), 13–32.

25. Howard McCurdy, "Selecting and Training Public Managers: Business Skills versus Public Administration," *Public Administration Review*, 38 (Nov./Dec. 1978), 571–578 (quote on p. 577).

26. William Leiserson, "The Theory of Public Employment Offices and the Principles of Their Practical Administration," *Political Science Quarterly*, 29 (Mar. 1914), 28–46.

27. Henry Hunt, "Obstacles to Municipal Progress," *American Political Science Review*, 11 (Feb. 1917), 76–87. Hunt equates a total reliance on businesslike efficiency with machine government; the machine's supporters are seen as believing democracy takes too long and has too many factions to make instrumental progress, and therefore they are willing to have the businesslike boss usurp power and get things done.

28. Henry Bruere, *The New City Government* (New York: D. Appleton and Co., 1912), 1.

29. The outline appears in "Instruction in Public Business."

30. This theme runs through most Bureau literature; see, for example, Allen "Instruction in Public Business."

31. The two Bureau-related works that assert the closest similarity between business and public administration are Cleveland, "Municipal Ownership" and Charles A. Beard, *The Administration and Politics of Tokyo* (New

York: Macmillan, 1923). However, both Cleveland (p. 363) and Beard (p. 22) make clear that the similarities are only in the nature of discrete activities; both men realize that goals and control mechanisms are dissimilar and that techniques must be appropriated from business with this in mind.

32. Allen, *Efficient Democracy*, ix.

33. Waldo, *The Administrative State* (New York: Ronald, 1948), 202.

34. Bureau of City Betterment, 3.

35. Frederick Cleveland, "The Need for Coordinating Municipal, State and National Activities," *Annals*, 41 (May 1912), 23–39 (quote on p. 27).

36. William Prendergast, "Efficiency through Accounting," *Annals*, 41 (May 1912), 43–56.

37. Henry Bruere, "Efficiency in City Government," *Annals*, 41 (May 1912), 1–22.

38. Bruere, *New City Government*, 112.

39. Allen, "Reminiscences," vol. 4, 525.

40. Bruere, *New City Government*, 108.

41. Robert Goodin and Peter Wilenski, "Beyond Efficiency: The Logical Underpinnings of Administrative Principles," *Public Administration Review* (Nov./Dec. 1984), 512–517.

42. "Cleveland Application of Scientific Management."

43. Henry Bruere, "Public Utilities Regulation in New York," *Annals*, 37 (Mar. 1908), 535–551 (quote on p. 537).

44. Beard, *American City Government*, 96.

45. Arthur Okun, *Equality and Efficiency: The Big Tradeoff* (Washington, D.C.: Brookings Institution, 1975); Orion White, Jr., "The Dialectical Organization: An Alternative to Bureaucracy," *Public Administration Review*, 29 (Jan./Feb. 1969), 32–42; Peter Wilenski, "Equity or Efficiency: Competing Values in Administration," *Policy Studies Journal*, 9 (1980), 1239–1249.

A succinct analysis of some of the possible trade-offs is offered in James Q. Wilson, "The Bureaucracy Problem," in *Urban Politics and Public Policy*, Stephen David and Paul Peterson, eds. (New York: Praeger, 1973), 27–34.

46. Carl Kelsey, "Review of William Allen's *Efficient Democracy*," *Annals*, 36 (July 1907), 171.

47. Terry Cooper, "Citizenship and Professionalism in Public Administration," *Public Administration Review*, 44, special issue (Mar. 1984), 143–149

(quote on p. 147). Again, no citations to municipal reform literature are given; they are all to modern summaries of this literature.

48. Beard, *American City Government*, 96, and *Administration and Politics of Tokyo*, 19.

49. Waldo, *Administrative State*, pp. 178–179.

50. Hindy Lauer Schachter, "Educating Policy Analysts," *News for Teachers of Political Science*, no. 44 (Winter 1985), 1–3.

51. Snedden and Allen, 5–6. See also pp. 116 and 142. In a 1949 manuscript, Bruere asserts that he was more aware than Allen of the need to interpret facts. Since Allen actually articulates this caution more explicitly, it is difficult to know how to read Bruere's assertion. Bruere may have refrained from articulating his doubts because he wanted statistics collected; this supposition supports the idea that Bureau writers deliberately downplayed the interpretation problem, assuming it could be raised when data collection had become an established policy. Henry Bruere, "Reminiscences," Mar.–May 1949, unpublished manuscript in Columbia University's Oral History Collection.

52. Waldo, *Administrative State*, ch. 6.

53. For an analysis of workplace experience as a source of political learning, see J. Maxwell Elden, "Political Efficacy at Work: The Connection between More Autonomous Forms of Workplace Organization and a More Participatory Politics," *American Political Science Review*, 75 (Mar. 1981), 43–58.

54. Henry Bruere, "The Future of the Police Arm from an Engineering Standpoint," *American Society of Mechanical Engineers Transactions*, 36 (1914), 535–547 (quote on pp. 546–547).

55. See the truly authoritarian standpoint of Reginald Bolton, "Discussion," *American Society of Mechanical Engineers Transactions*, 36 (1914), 547.

56. Graham, 135.

57. Dahlberg, 42, 129. Taylor spoke several times to Training School students (p. 144).

58. Allen, "Reminiscences," vol. 1, p. 46. See also William Allen, "Training Men and Women for Public Service," *Annals*, 41 (May 1912), 307–312.

59. Committee of Seven, American Political Science Association, "Report of Committee of Seven on Instruction in Colleges and Universities," *American Political Science Review*, 9 (May 1915), 353–374.

60. Leonard White, *Introduction to the Study of Public Administration* (New York: Macmillan, 1926). Second, third, and fourth editions appeared

in 1939, 1948, and 1955, respectively. For comments on the impact of the books, see Herbert Storing, "Leonard D. White and the Study of Public Administration," *Public Administration Review*, 25 (Mar. 1965), 38–51.

61. Leonard White, *Conditions of Municipal Employment in Chicago: A Study of Morale*, report submitted to the Chicago City Council, June 10, 1925, available at the Institute of Public Administration, New York City.

62. White, *Introduction* (1926), ch. 1.

63. William F. Willoughby, *Principles of Public Administration* (Baltimore: John Hopkins Press, 1927), Preface.

64. John Pfiffner, *Public Administration* (New York: Ronald Press, 1935), and *Research Methods in Public Administration* (New York: Ronald Press, 1940).

65. The term "new public administration" occurs in Pfiffner, *Public Administration*, 5–6.

66. Particularly in *Research Methods in Public Administration*, 112, where Pfiffner uses Taylor's work to call for action-oriented research.

67. Pfiffner, *Public Administration*, 496–497.

68. *Research Methods in Public Administration*, 25.

69. Elton Mayo, *The Human Problems of an Industrial Civilization* (New York: Viking, 1933); F. J. Roethlisberger and William Dickson, *Management and the Worker* (Cambridge, Mass.: Harvard University Press, 1939); and F. J. Roethlisberger, *Management and Morale* (Cambridge, Mass.: Harvard University Press, 1941).

70. See, for example, Mayo, 172, Roethlisberger and Dickson, 545–546; and Roethlisberger, 24.

71. White, *Conditions of Municipal Employment in Chicago*, particularly 40–43.

72. L. J. Henderson, T. N. Whitehead, and Elton Mayo, "The Effects of Social Environment," in *Papers on the Science of Administration*, Luther Gulick and Lyndall Urwick, eds. (New York: Institute of Public Administration, 1937), 143–158.

73. Luther Gulick, "Foreward," in Gulick and Urwick, v.

74. Gulick makes this explicit in his "Beard and Municipal Reform," 57.

75. Luther Gulick, "Notes on the Theory of Organization," in Gulick and Urwick, 1–45 (quote on p. 6). See also the analysis of this piece in

Thomas H. Hammond, "In Defense of Luther Gulick's 'Notes on the Theory of Organization.' " *Public Administration* (forthcoming).

Chapter 8: Scientific Management and Public Administration: Act Two

1. Robert Dahl, "The Science of Public Administration: Three Problems," *Public Administration Review*, (Winter 1947), 1–11.

2. The shift is reflected in the change in the chapter where textbooks discuss scientific management. Prior to World War II, Taylor is discussed in chapters on the aim and scope of the discipline. After Dahl's article, most of the major textbooks discuss Taylor in relation to motivation or personnel management, although a few still also discuss his overall work in an introductory chapter.

3. Dahl, 6, note 16.

4. For Waldo's impressions of the book's reception and message, see Brack Brown and Richard Stillman II, *A Search for Public Administration: The Ideas and Career of Dwight Waldo* (College Station: Texas A&M University Press, 1986).

5. Dwight Waldo, "The Administrative State Revisited," *Public Administration Review*, 25 (Mar. 1965), 5–30.

6. Arthur Macmahon, "Review of Dwight Waldo, *The Administrative State*, and Joseph Goldfarb, *Freedom and the Administrative State*," *Public Administration Review* (Summer 1948), 203–211.

7. Herbert Simon, Donald Smithburg, and Victor Thompson, *Public Administration* (New York: Knopf, 1950), 570.

8. Merrill Collett, "Strategy versus Tactics as the Object of Research in Public Administration," *Public Administration Review*, 22 (Sept. 1962), 115–120 (quote on p. 117).

9. Elton Mayo, *The Human Problems of an Industrial Civilization* (New York: Viking, 1933), 177.

10. F. J. Roethlisberger, *Management and Morale* (Cambridge, Mass.: Harvard University Press, 1941), 166.

11. Roethlisberger, 181.

12. F. J. Roethlisberger and William Dickson, *Management and the Worker* (Cambridge, Mass.: Harvard University Press, 1939), 532–533.

13. Robert Miewald, *Public Administration* (New York: McGraw-Hill, 1978), 197.

14. A. Lawrence Lowell, "The Physiology of Politics," *American Political Science Review*, 4 (Feb. 1910), 1–15.

15. For an explication of the contrasting relations of the natural sciences and the arts to the lay public in terms of language, see Thomas Kuhn, *The Structure of Scientific Revolutions*, 2nd ed. (Chicago: University of Chicago Press, 1970), 164.

16. Daniel Wren and Robert Hay, "Management Historians and Business Historians: Differing Perceptions of Pioneer Contributors," *Academy of Management Journal*, 20 (Sept. 1977), 470–475.

17. For example, see, Frederick Taylor to Morris Cooke, Sept. 12, 1906, and Jan. 7, 1910, where he stresses using narrative and short Anglo-Saxon words to convince the average person. (Taylor Collection).

18. See, for example, Luther Gulick's portrait of this aspect of Beard's work in "Beard and Municipal Reform," in *Charles Beard*, Howard Beale, ed. (Lexington: University of Kentucky Press, 1954), 47–60.

19. Frederick Taylor, *Shop Management* (1903) (New York: Harper and Brothers, 1947), 21.

20. Peter Drucker, "The Coming Rediscovery of Scientific Management," *Conference Board Record* (June 1976), 23–27; Louis Fry, "The Maligned F. W. Taylor," *Academy of Management Review*, 1 (July, 1976), 124–129; Edwin Locke, "The Ideas of Frederick Taylor: An Evaluation," *Academy of Management Review*, 7 (1982), 14–24.

21. He even says efficiency is weakened because "management is not yet looked upon as an art, with laws as exact . . . as the fundamental principles of engineering, which demand long and careful thought and study." *Shop Management*, 18.

22. The major essays of this movement are in Frank Marini, ed., *Towards a New Public Administration: The Minnowbrook Perspective* and Dwight Waldo, ed., *Public Administration in a Time of Turbulence* (Scranton, Pa.: Chandler, 1971). An analysis of the "new" public administration appears in H. George Frederickson, *New Public Administration* (University: University of Alabama Press, 1980).

Bibliography

I. Published Material

Aitken, Hugh. *Taylorism at Watertown Arsenal*. Cambridge, Mass.: Harvard University Press, 1960.

Allen, William. *Efficient Democracy*. New York: Dodd, Mead and Co., 1907.

_____. "Instruction in Public Business." *Political Science Quarterly*, 22 (1908), 604–616.

_____. "Training Men and Women for Public Service," *Annals*, 41 (May 1912), 307–312.

Allison, Graham, Jr. "Public and Private Management: Are They Fundamentally Alike in All Unimportant Respects?", in *Current Issues in Public Administration*, Frederick Lane, ed., 2nd ed. New York: St. Martin's Press, 1982.

"American Society of Mechanical Engineers," *Engineering*, 52 (July 3, 1891), 17.

Argyris, Chris. "Some Limits of Rational Man Organizational Theory." *Public Administration Review*, 33 (May/June, 1973), 253–267.

Barnard, Chester I. *The Functions of the Executive*. Cambridge, Mass.: Harvard University Press, 1938.

Barnes, Barry. *Interests and the Growth of Knowledge*. London: Routledge and Kegan Paul, 1977.

_____. *T. S. Kuhn and Social Science*. New York: Columbia University Press, 1982.

Beard, Charles. *The Administration and Politics of Tokyo*. New York: Macmillan, 1923.

_____. *American City Government*. New York: Century Company, 1912.

_____. *An Economic Interpretation of the Constitution of the United States*. New York: Macmillan, 1913.

Berkley, George. *The Craft of Public Administration*, 3rd ed. Boston: Allyn and Bacon, 1981.

Bettelheim, Bruno. *Freud and Man's Soul*. New York: Knopf, 1983.

Blume, Stuart. *Towards a Political Sociology of Science*. New York: Free Press, 1974.

Bolton, Reginald. "Discussion." *American Society of Mechanical Engineers Transactions*, 36 (1914), 547.

Brandeis, Louis D. "Address," in *Frederick Winslow Taylor: A Memorial Volume*. New York: Taylor Society, 1920.

_____. *Business—A Profession*. Boston: Small, Maynard and Co., 1914.

_____. "Foreword," in Frank Gilbreth, *Primer of Scientific Management*. Easton, Penn.: Hive Publishing Co., 1973 (originally published in 1914).

Brown, Brack and Richard Stillman II. *A Search for Public Administration: The Ideas and Career of Dwight Waldo*. College Station: Texas A & M University Press, 1986.

Brown, Ernest. "The Response of Workers to Scientific Management," in *Scientific Management in American Industry*, Harlow Person, ed. New York: Harper and Brothers, 1929.

Bruere, Henry. "Efficiency in City Government." *Annals*, 41 (May 1912), 1–22.

_____. "The Future of the Police Arm from an Engineering Standpoint." *American Society of Mechanical Engineers Transactions*, 36 (1914), 535–547.

_____. *The New City Government*. New York: D. Appleton and Co., 1912.

_____. "Public Utilities Regulation in New York." *Annals*, 37 (Mar. 1908), 535–551.

Bureau of City Betterment of the Citizens Union of New York. *The Police Problem in New York City.* New York: Citizens Union, 1906.

Burlingham, Charles. "Introduction," David Snedden and William Allen, *School Reports and School Efficiency.* New York: Macmillan, 1908.

Caiden, Gerald. "In Search of an Apolitical Science of American Public Administration," in *Politics and Administration: Woodrow Wilson and American Public Administration,* Jack Rabin and James Bowman, eds. New York: Marcel Dekker, 1984.

Church, A. "Discussion." *American Society of Mechanical Engineers Transactions,* 34 (1912), 1158.

Cleveland, Frederick. "Municipal Ownership as a Form of Governmental Control." *Annals,* 35 (1906), 359–370.

———. "The Need for Coordinating Municipal, State and National Activities." *Annals,* 41 (May 1912), 25–39.

———. *Organized Democracy.* New York: Longmans, Green and Co., 1913.

Cleveland, Frederick with the assistance of Clarence Smith. *Principles of Government Organization and Management.* Washington, D.C.: Army Education Commission, 1919.

Cleveland, Harlan. "The Twilight of Hierarchy: Speculations on the Global Information Society." *Public Administration Review,* 45 (Jan./Feb. 1985), 185–195.

Collett, Merrill. "Strategy versus Tactics as the Object of Research in Public Administration." *Public Administration Review,* 22 (Sept. 1962), 115–120.

Committee of Seven, American Political Science Association. "Report of Committee of Seven on Instruction in Colleges and Universities." *American Political Science Review,* 9 (May 1915), 353–374.

Cooke, Morris. *How about It?* Lancaster, Penn.: New Era Printing Co., 1917.

———. *Our Cities Awake.* New York: Doubleday, Page and Co., 1918.

———. *Snapping Cords: Comments on the Changing Attitudes of American Cities.* Privately printed, 1915.

_____. "Some Factors in Municipal Engineering." *American Society of Mechanical Engineers Transactions*, 36 (1914), 605–618.

_____. "Who Is Boss in Your Shop?" *Annals*, 71 (May 1917), 167–185.

Cooper, Terry. "Citizenship and Professionalism in Public Administration." *Public Administration Review*, 44, special issue (Mar. 1984), 143–149.

Copley, Frank. *Frederick W. Taylor*. 2 vols. New York: Harper and Brothers, 1923.

Dahl, Robert. "The Science of Public Administration: Three Problems." *Public Administration Review*, 7 (Winter 1947), 1–11.

Dahlberg, Jane. *The New York Bureau of Municipal Research*. New York: New York University Press, 1966.

Dimock, Marshall, Gladys Ogden Dimock, and Douglas Fox. *Public Administration*, 5th ed. New York: Holt, Rinehart and Winston, 1983.

Doig, Jameson. " 'If I See a Murderous Fellow Sharpening a Knife Cleverly . . . ': The Wilsonian Dichotomy and the Public Authority Tradition." *Public Administration Review*, 43 (July/Aug. 1983), 292–304.

Drucker, Peter. "The Coming Rediscovery of Scientific Management." *Conference Board Record* (June 1976), 25–37.

Dulles, Foster Rhea and Melvyn Dubofsky. *Labor in America, A History*, 4th ed. Arlington Heights, Ill.: Harlan Davidson, 1984.

Dunaway, J. A. "Standardization and Inspection." *American Political Science Review*, 10 (May 1916), 315–319.

Easton, David. *A Framework for Political Analysis*. Englewood Cliffs, N. J.: Prentice-Hall, 1965.

Economic Studies. Vol. 1 (Apr. 1896).

Elden, J. Maxwell. "Political Efficacy at Work: The Connection between More Autonomous Forms of Workplace Organization and a More Participatory Politics." *American Political Science Review*, 75 (Mar. 1981), 43–58.

Etzioni, Amitai. *Modern Organizations*. Englewood Cliffs, N. J.: Prentice-Hall, 1964.

Evidence Taken by the Interstate Commerce Commission in the Matter of Proposed Advances in Freight Rates by Carriers. U.S. Senate Doc. 725, 61st Congress, 3rd Sess. Washington, D.C.: U. S. Government Printing Office, 1911.

Frederickson, H. George. *New Public Administration.* University: University of Alabama Press, 1980.

Fry, Louis. "The Maligned F. W. Taylor: A Reply to His Many Critics." *Academy of Management Review,* 1 (July 1976), 124–129.

Gadamer, Hans Georg. *Truth and Method,* Garrett Bardin and John Cumming, trans., 2nd ed. New York: Seabury, 1975.

Gantt, Henry. "Discussion." *American Society of Mechanical Engineers Transactions,* 34 (1912), 1165.

————. "Training Workmen in Habits of Industry and Cooperation." *American Society of Mechanical Engineers Transactions,* 30 (1908), 1037–1048.

Goldberg, Joseph and William Moye. *The First Hundred Years of the Bureau of Labor Statistics.* Washington, D.C.: U.S. Department of Labor, 1984.

Goodin, Robert and Peter Wilenski. "Beyond Efficiency: The Logical Underpinnings of Administrative Principles." *Public Administration Review* (Nov./Dec. 1984), 512–517.

Goodnow, Frank. *Politics and Administration.* New York: Russell and Russell, 1900.

Goodsell, Charles. "Charles A. Beard, Prophet for Public Administration." *Public Administration Review,* 46 (Mar./Apr. 1986), 105–107.

Gordon, George. *Public Administration in America,* 2nd ed. New York: St. Martin's Press, 1982.

Gortner, Harold. *Administration in the Public Sector,* 2nd ed. New York: Wiley, 1981.

Graham, George. *Education for Public Administration.* Chicago: Public Administration Service, 1941.

Greenwood, Ronald, Alfred Bolton, and Regina Greenwood. "Hawthorne a Half Century Later: Relay Assembly Participants Remember," in *Readings and Study Guide for Management,* Jane Whitney Gibson, Regina Greenwood, and Ronald Greenwood, eds. Orlando, Fla.: Academy Press, 1985, 27–35.

Guerreiro Ramos, Albert. "Misplacements of Concepts and Administrative Theory." *Public Administration Review* (Nov./Dec. 1978), 550–557.

_____. "Models of Man and Administrative Theory," *Public Administration Review* (May/June 1972), 241–246.

Gulick, Luther. "Beard and Municipal Reform," in *Charles Beard*, Howard Beale, ed. Lexington: University of Kentucky Press, 1954.

_____. "Foreward," in *Papers on the Science of Administration*, Luther Gulick and Lyndall Urwick, eds. New York: Institute of Public Administration, 1937.

_____. "Notes on the Theory of Organization," in *Papers on the Science of Administration*, Luther Gulick and Lyndall Urwick, eds. New York: Institute of Public Administration, 1937.

Halsey, Frank. "Discussion." *American Society of Mechanical Engineers Transactions*, 16 (1895), 885.

_____. "Premium Plan of Paying for Labor." *American Society of Mechanical Engineers Transactions*, 12 (1891), 755–764.

Hamilton, Alexander. "Federalist Paper No. 11" in *Selections from The Federalist*, Henry Commanger, ed. New York: Appleton-Century-Crofts, 1949.

Hammond, Thomas. "In Defense of Luther Gulick's 'Notes on the Theory of Organization'." *Public Administration* (forthcoming).

Harmon, Michael and Richard Mayer. *Organization Theory for Public Administrators*. Boston: Little, Brown and Co., 1986.

Haskell, Thomas. *The Emergence of Professional Social Science: The American Social Science Association and the Nineteenth-Century Crisis of Authority*. Urbana: University of Illinois Press, 1977.

Hawkins, John. "Discussion." *American Society of Mechanical Engineers Transactions*, 12 (1891), 773.

_____. "Discussion." *American Society of Mechanical Engineers Transactions*, 24 (1903), 1460–1461.

Henderson, L. J., T. N. Whitehead and Elton Mayo. "The Effects of Social Environment," in *Papers on the Science of Administration*, Luther Gulick and Lyndall Urwick, eds. New York: Institute of Public Administration, 1937.

Henning, Gustavus. "Discussion." *American Society of Mechanical Engineers Transactions*, 16 (1895), 893–894.

Henry, Nicholas. *Public Administration and Public Affairs*. Englewood Cliffs, N. J.: Prentice-Hall, 1975.

Herson, Lawrence. *The Politics of Ideas: Political Theory and American Public Policy*. Homewood, Ill.: Dorsey, 1984.

Hill, Larry and F. Ted Hebert. *Essentials of Public Administration: A Text with Readings*. North Scituate, Mass.: Duxbury Press, 1979.

Hofstadter, Richard. *The Age of Reform: From Bryan to FDR*. New York: Alfred Knopf, 1959.

————. *The Progressive Historians*. New York: Alfred Knopf, 1968.

Hoxie, Robert. *Scientific Management and Labor*. New York: Augustus Kelly, 1966 (originally published in 1915).

Hudson, Frank. "The Machinist's Side of Taylorism." *American Machinist* (Apr. 27, 1911), 773.

Hunt, Henry. "Obstacles to Municipal Progress." *American Political Science Review*, 11 (Feb. 1917), 76–87.

International Association of Machinists. *Official Circular*, no. 12, Apr. 26, 1911 (Taylor Collection).

Jun, Jong. *Public Administration: Design and Problem Solving*. New York: Macmillan, 1986.

Kakar, Sudhir. *Frederick Taylor: A Study in Personality and Innovation*. Cambridge, Mass.: MIT Press, 1970.

Kaufman, Herbert. "Emerging Conflicts in the Doctrines of Public Administration." *American Political Science Review*, 50 (Dec. 1956), 1057–1073.

Kelsey, Carl. "Review of William Allen's *Efficient Democracy*." *Annals*, 36 (July 1907), 171.

Kent, William. "Discussion." *American Society of Mechanical Engineers Transactions*, 30 (1908), 1061.

Kolko, Gabriel. *The Triumph of Conservatism*. New York: Free Press, 1963.

Korman, Gerd. *Industrialization, Immigrants and Americanizers*. Madison: Historical Society of Wisconsin, 1967.

Kraemer, Kenneth and John Leslie King. "Computing and Public Organizations." *Public Administration Review*, 46 (Nov. 1986), 488–496.

Kramer, Fred. *Dynamics of Public Bureaucracy*, 2nd ed. Cambridge, Mass.: Winthrop, 1981.

Kuhn, Thomas. *The Structure of Scientific Revolutions*, 2nd ed. Chicago: University of Chicago Press, 1970.

Larson, Magali Sarfati. *The Rise of Professionalism*. Berkeley and Los Angeles: University of California Press, 1977.

Laudon, Kenneth. *Computers and Bureaucratic Reform*. New York: Wiley, 1974.

Layton, Edwin, Jr. *The Revolt of the Engineers: Social Responsibility and the American Engineering Profession*. Cleveland, Ohio: Case Western Reserve University Press, 1971.

Leiserson, Avery. "The Study of Public Administration," in *Elements of Public Administration*, Fritz Morstein Marx, ed. Englewood Cliffs, N. J.: Prentice-Hall, 1946.

Leiserson, William. "The Theory of Public Employment Offices and the Principles of Their Practical Administration." *Political Science Quarterly*, 29 (Mar. 1914), 28–46.

Locke, Edwin. "The Ideas of Frederick Taylor: An Evaluation." *Academy of Management Review*, 7 (1982), 14–24.

Lowell, A. Lawrence. "The Physiology of Politics." *American Political Science Review*, 4 (Feb. 1910), 1–15.

_____. *Public Opinion and Popular Government*. New York: Longmans, Green and Company, 1913.

Lutrin, Carl and Allen Settle. *American Public Administration: Concepts and Cases*, 3rd ed. Englewood Cliffs, N. J.: Prentice-Hall, 1985.

Macmahon, Arthur. "Review of Dwight Waldo, *The Administrative State*, and Joseph Goldfarb, *Freedom and the Administrative State*." *Public Administration Review*, 7 (Summer 1948), 203–211.

March, James and Herbert Simon. *Organizations.* New York: Wiley, 1958.

Marini, Frank, ed. *Towards a New Public Administration: The Minnowbrook Perspective.* Scranton, Penn.: Chandler, 1971.

Martin, Daniel. "The Fading Legacy of Woodrow Wilson." *Public Administration Review,* 48 (Mar./Apr. 1988), 631–636.

Maslow, Abraham. *Motivation and Personality.* New York: Harper and Row, 1954.

––––––. *The Further Reaches of Human Nature.* New York: Viking, 1971.

Mason, Alpheus. *Brandeis: A Free Man's Life.* New York: Viking, 1946.

Mayo, Elton. *The Human Problems of an Industrial Civilization.* New York: Viking, 1933.

McCurdy, Howard. *Public Administration: A Synthesis.* Menlo Park, Calif.: Cummings Publishing Co., 1977.

––––––. "Selecting and Training Public Managers: Business Skills versus Public Administration." *Public Administration Review,* 38 (Nov./Dec. 1978), 571–578.

McGregor, Douglas. *The Human Side of Enterprise.* New York: McGraw-Hill, 1960.

Merriam, Charles and Harold Lasswell. "Current Public Opinion and the Public Service Commission," in *Public Utility Regulation,* Morris Cooke, ed. New York: Ronald Press, 1924.

Merton, Robert. *The Sociology of Science: Theoretical and Empirical Investigations.* Chicago: University of Chicago Press, 1973.

Metcalfe, Henry. *The Cost of Manufactures and the Administration of Workshops Public and Private.* New York: John Wiley and Sons, 1885.

––––––. "The Shop Order System of Accounts." *American Society of Mechanical Engineers Transactions,* 7 (1886), 440–448.

Miewald, Robert. *Public Administration.* New York: McGraw-Hill, 1978.

Morgan, David. *Managing Urban America.* North Scituate, Mass.: Duxbury Press, 1979.

Morgan, Gareth. *Images of Organizations*. Beverly Hills, Calif.: Sage, 1986.

Mulkay, Michael. *Science and the Sociology of Knowledge*. London: George Allen and Unwin, 1979.

————. *The Social Process of Innovation: A Study in the Sociology of Science*. London: Macmillan, 1972.

Nadworny, Milton. *Scientific Management and the Unions, 1900–1932*. Cambridge, Mass.: Harvard University Press, 1955.

Nelson, Daniel. *Frederick W. Taylor and the Rise of Scientific Management*. Madison: University of Wisconsin Press, 1980.

————*Managers and Workers: Origins of the New Factory System in the United States, 1880–1920*. Madison: University of Wisconsin Press, 1975.

Noble, David. *Forces of Production: A Social History of Industrial Automation*. New York: Knopf, 1984.

O'Daniel, Edgar. "Review of Frederick Taylor's *Principles of Scientific Management*." *Political Science Quarterly*, 3 (1912), 534–536.

Okun, Arthur. *Equality and Efficiency: The Big Tradeoff*. Washington, D.C.: Brookings Institution, 1975.

Parsons, H. McIlvaine. "What Caused the Hawthorne Effect? A Scientific Detective Story." *Administration and Society*, 10 (1978), 259–284.

Partridge, William. "Capital's Need for High-Priced Labor," *American Society of Mechanical Engineers Transactions*, 8 (1887), 269–275.

Person, Harlow. "The Origin and Nature of Scientific Management," in *Scientific Management in American Industry*, Harlow Person, ed. New York: Harper and Brothers, 1929.

Pfiffner, John. *Public Administration*. New York: Ronald Press, 1935.

————. *Research Methods in Public Administration*. New York: Ronald Press, 1940.

Polanyi, Michael. *Science, Faith and Society*. Chicago: University of Chicago Press, 1964.

Prendergast, William. "Efficiency through Accounting." *Annals*, 41 (May 1912), 43–56.

Preston, Larry. "Freedom and Bureaucracy." *American Journal of Political Science*, 31 (Nov. 1987), 773–795.

"Privatization: Limits and Applications," *Public Administration Review*, 47 (Nov./Dec. 1987), 453–484.

Pursley, Robert and Neil Snortland. *Managing Government Organizations: An Introduction to Public Administration*. North Scituate, Mass.: Duxbury Press, 1980.

Ricci, David. *The Tragedy of Political Science: Politics, Scholarship and Democracy*. New Haven, Conn.: Yale University Press, 1984.

Ricoeur, Paul. "The Model of the Text: Meaningful Action Considered as a Text." *Social Research*, 38 (1971), 529–562.

Roethlisberger, F. J. *Management and Morale*. Cambridge, Mass.: Harvard University Press, 1941.

Roethlisberger, F. J. and William Dickson. *Management and the Worker*. Cambridge, Mass.: Harvard University Press, 1939.

Rosenbloom, David. "Public Administrative Theory and the Separation of Powers." *Public Administration Review*, 43 (May/June 1983), 219–226.

Sabia, Daniel, Jr. "Political Education and the History of Political Thought." *American Political Science Review*, 78 (Dec. 1984), 985–999.

Schachter, Hindy Lauer. "Educating Policy Analysts." *News for Teachers of Political Science*, no. 44 (Winter 1985), 1–3.

Schelling, Thomas. *The Strategy of Conflict*. Cambridge, Mass.: Harvard University Press, 1960.

Scott, William and David Hart. "Administrative Crisis: The Neglect of Metaphysical Speculation." *Public Administration Review* (Sept./Oct. 1973), 415–422.

Shaiken, Harley. *Work Transformed: Automation and Labor in the Golden Age*. Lexington, Mass.: D.C. Heath, 1986.

Sharkansky, Ira. *Public Administration: Policy-Making in Government Agencies*, 4th ed. Chicago: Rand-McNally, 1978.

Simon, Herbert. "Organization Man: Rational or Self-Actualizing?" *Public Administration Review*, 33 (July/August 1973), 346–353.

Simon, Herbert, Donald Smithburg, and Victor Thompson. *Public Administration*. New York: Alfred Knopf, 1950.

Skinner, Quentin. "Meaning and Understanding in the History of Ideas." *History and Theory*, 8 (1969), 3–53.

Sklar, Martin. "Woodrow Wilson and the Political Economy of Modern U.S. Liberalism," in *For a New America: Essays in History and Politics from Studies on the Left, 1959–1967*, James Weinstein and David Eakins, eds. New York: Random House, 1970.

Smith, Merritt Roe. *Harpers Ferry Armory and the New Technology: The Challenge of Change*. Ithaca, N. Y.; Cornell University Press, 1977.

Snedden, David and William Allen. *School Reports and School Efficiency*. New York: Macmillan, 1908.

Somit, Albert and Joseph Tanenhaus. *The Development of American Political Science*. Boston: Allyn and Bacon, 1967.

Stone, Alice and Donald Stone. "Early Development of Education in Public Administration," in *American Public Administration: Past, Present, Future*, Frederick Mosher, ed. University: University of Alabama Press, 1975.

Storing, Herbert. "Leonard D. White and the Study of Public Administration." *Public Administration Review*, XXV (March, 1965), 38–51.

Straussman, Jeffrey. *Public Administration*. New York: Holt, Rinehart and Winston, 1985.

Sub-Committee on Administration. "The Present State of the Art of Industrial Management." *American Society of Mechanical Engineers Transactions*, 34 (1912), 1140–1147.

Tarbell, Ida. "The Golden Rule in Business." *American Magazine* (November, 1914), 11–17.

_____. "The Golden Rule in Business: His Own Worst Enemy," *American Magazine* (May, 1915), 20–23, 94, 98.

_____. "The Golden Rule in Business: Making the Hire Worthy of the Laborer." *American Magazine* (February, 1915), 25–29, 66.

Taylor, Frederick. "A Piece-Rate System Being a Step Toward Partial Solution of the Labor Problem." *American Society of Mechanical Engineers Transactions*, 16 (1895), 856–883.

Taylor, Frederick. *Shop Management*. New York: Harper and Brothers, 1947 (originally published in 1903).

———. *The Principles of Scientific Management*. New York: Harper and Brothers, 1947 (originally published in 1911).

———. *Testimony before the Special House Committee*. New York: Harper and Brothers, 1947 (originally published in 1912).

———. "Why Manufacturers Dislike College Graduates." *Proceedings of the Society for the Promotion of Engineering Education*. Ithaca, N. Y.: Cornell University, 1909.

Thayer, Frederick. *An End to Hierarchy and Competition*, 2nd ed. New York: Franklin Watts, 1981.

———. "Productivity: Taylorism Revisited (Round Three)." *Public Administration Review*, 32 (Nov./Dec. 1972), 833–840.

Towne, Henry. "The Engineer as an Economist." *American Society of Mechanical Engineers Transactions*, 7 (1886), 428–432.

———. "Gain Sharing." *American Society of Mechanical Engineers Transactions*, 10 (1888), 600–614.

Trilling, Lionel. *The Experience of Literature*. New York: Holt, Rinehart and Winston, 1969.

Trombley, Kenneth. *The Life and Times of a Happy Liberal: A Biography of Morris Llewellyn Cooke*. New York: Harper and Brothers, 1954.

"Union Hears of Brandeis Idea." *Boston Herald*, Apr. 3, 1911.

United States House of Representatives, Committee to Investigate U.S. Steel Corporation. *Hearings*. Washington, D.C.: U.S. Government Printing Office, 1912.

United States House of Representatives, Labor Committee. *Hearings before the Committee on Labor*. Washington, D.C.: U.S. Government Printing Office, 1911.

————. *Hearings on a Bill to Prevent the Use of the Stop Watch.* Washington, D.C.: U.S. Government Printing Office, 1914.

United States House of Representatives, Special Committee to Investigate the Taylor and Other Systems of Shop Management. *Hearings.* 3 vols. Washington, D.C.: U.S. Government Printing Office, 1912.

Waldo, Dwight. *The Administrative State.* New York: Ronald Press, 1948.

————. "The Administrative State Revisited." *Public Administration Review,* 25 (Mar. 1965), 5–30.

————. (ed.). *Public Administration in a Time of Turbulence.* Scranton, Penn.: Chandler, 1971.

White, Leonard. *Introduction to the Study of Public Administration,* 1st ed. New York: Macmillan, 1926.

White, Orion, Jr. "The Dialectical Organization: An Alternative to Bureaucracy." *Public Administration Review,* 29 (Jan./Feb. 1969), 32–42.

Whittier, John Greenleaf. "The Saddest Words," in *The New Pocket Anthology of American Verse,* Oscar Williams, ed. New York: Washington Square Press, 1961.

Wilenski, Peter. "Equity or Efficiency: Competing Values in Administration." *Policy Studies Journal,* 9 (1980), 1239–1249.

Willoughby, William F. *Principles of Public Administration.* Baltimore: John Hopkins Press, 1927.

Wilson, James Q. "The Bureaucracy Problem," in *Urban Politics and Public Policy,* Stephen David and Paul Peterson, eds. New York: Praeger, 1973.

Wilson, Woodrow. "The Study of Public Administration." *Political Science Quarterly,* 2 (June 1887), 197–222.

Wolin, Sheldon. "Political Theory as a Vocation." *American Political Science Review,* 63 (Dec. 1969), 1062–1080.

————. *Politics and Vision.* Boston: Little, Brown, and Co., 1960.

Wrege, Charles and A. Perroni. "Taylor's Pig-Tale: A Historical Analysis of Frederick W. Taylor's Pig-Iron Experiments." *Academy of Management Journal,* 17 (1974), 6–27.

Wrege, Charles and A. Stotka. "Cooke Creates a Classic: The Story behind F. W. Taylor's Principles of Scientific Management." *Academy of Management Review*, 3 (Oct. 1978), 736–749.

Wren, Daniel. *The Evolution of Management Thought*, 2d ed. New York: Wiley, 1979.

Wren, Daniel and Robert Hay. "Management Historians and Business Historians: Differing Perceptions of Pioneer Contributors." *Academy of Management Journal*, 20 (Sept. 1977), 470–475.

Yeager, Samuel, Jack Rabin, and Thomas Vocino. "Feedback and Administrative Behavior in the Public Sector." *Public Administration Review*, 45 (Sept./Oct. 1985), 570–575.

Ziman, John. *Public Knowledge*. London: Cambridge University Press, 1968.

Zuckerman, Harriet and Robert Merton. "Institutionalized Patterns of Evaluation in Science," in *The Sociology of Science*, Norman Storer, ed. Chicago: University of Chicago Press, 1973.

II. Unpublished Material

Papers, Reports, Reminiscences, and Dissertation

Allen, William. "Reminiscences." Dec. 1949–Feb. 1950. Unpublished manuscript in Oral History Collection, Columbia University.

Beard, Charles. "Philosophy, Science and Art of Public Administration." Paper presented to the Governmental Research Association, Princeton, N. J., Sept. 8, 1939. (New York Public Library).

Bruere, Henry. "Reminiscences." Mar.–May 1949. Unpublished manuscript in Oral History Collection, Columbia University.

Chipman, Miner. "Efficiency, Scientific Management and Organized Labor." Paper presented to the Efficiency Society, Jan. 21, 1916 (Taylor Collection).

Cleveland, Frederick. "The Application of Scientific Management to the Activities of the State." Paper presented at Dartmouth College, Oct. 18, 1912 (available at Institute of Public Administration, New York City).

Cooke, Morris. "Preface [to Frederick Taylor, *Principles of Scientific Management*]." Undated manuscript (Taylor Collection).

——. "Public Engineering and Human Progress." Paper presented to the Cleveland Engineering Society, November, 14, 1916 (New York Public Library).

——. "The Spirit and Social Significance of Scientific Management." Paper presented at the Western Economic Association Annual Meeting, Chicago, Mar. 14, 1913 (Taylor Collection).

Litterer, Joseph. "The Emergence of Systematic Management as Indicated by the Literature of Management from 1870 to 1900." Ph.D. dissertation, University of Illinois, 1959.

Person, Harlow. "Report of the Managing Director: A Decade of Progress." Unpublished Taylor Society Report, Feb. 5, 1926 (Cooke Collection).

"Public Policies to Municipal Utilities." Conference program, Nov. 12–14, 1914 (Taylor Collection).

Taylor, Frederick. "The Conservation of Human Effort." Paper presented to the City Club of Philadelphia, Jan. 8, 1911 (Taylor Collection).

——. "Government Efficiency." Unpublished manuscript (Taylor Collection).

Van Riper, Paul. "Administrative Thought in the 1880s: State of the Art." Paper presented at the American Society for Public Administration Annual Conference, Anaheim, Calif., Apr. 1986.

White, Leonard. *Conditions of Municipal Employment in Chicago: A Study of Morale.* Report submitted to the Chicago City Council, June 10, 1925 (available at Institute of Public Administration, New York City).

Letters and Memorandum

Barth, Carl to Frederick Taylor, Aug. 12, 1911.

Bolger, Eliot to Morris Cooke, Apr. 30, 1913.

Brandeis, Louis to (1) Morris Cooke, July 10, 1914; (2) Frederick Taylor, Oct. 26, 1910, Sept. 14, 1911.

Cleveland, Frederick to Morris Cooke, Sept. 29, 1922.

Cooke, Morris to (1) C. W. Baker, June 4, 1915; Jan. 3, 1916; (2) Rudolph Blankenberg, Jan. 30, 1913; (3) Samuel Bodine, Feb. 28, 1913; (4) Louis Brandeis, July 9, Oct. 15, 1914; (5) William Chantland, Sept. 13, 1928; (6) Frederick Cleveland, Sept. 6, 1921; Nov. 5, 1926; (7) Calvin Rice, Mar. 7, 1916; (8) Frederick Taylor, Feb. 5; Nov. 10, Dec. 10, 1910; Mar. 18, Dec. 22, 1911, July 23, Sept. 23, 1914; (9) Louise Taylor, Mar. 28, 1934; (10) Robert Wolf, May 25, 1922.

Faught, Albert Smith to Morris Cooke, Mar. 4, 1912.

Heydon, Charles to Birge Harrison, n.d.

King, Clyde to Frederick Taylor, Feb. 21, 1912.

Rice, Calvin to American Society of Mechanical Engineers Council members (memorandum), Mar. 3, 1915.

Smith, J. Russell to Frederick Taylor, Jan. 27, 1915.

Taylor, Frederick to (1) Louis Brandeis, n.d. (probably late Oct./early Nov., 1910); Apr. 15, 1911; (2) Morris Cooke, Sept. 12, 1906; Jan. 22, July 23, 1909; Jan. 7, 13, Mar. 29, May 5, Oct. 6, Dec. 2, 10, 1910; March 23, Aug. 20, Nov. 27, 1911; Sept. 2, 1914; (3) General William Crozier, June 9, 26, Sept. 21, 1911; (4) Edwin Gay, Oct. 9, 1913; (5) H. J. Porter, Nov. 6, 1911; (6) J. Russell Smith, Feb. 8, 1915; (7) C. Bertrand Thompson, Dec. 30, 1914 (8) E. C. Wolf, Mar. 11, 1915.

Index

Progressive movement (*cont.*)
and Frederick Taylor, 51–55; and
the utility companies, 84
Public administration: and business
administration, 75; growth as discipline 3, 71–72; and technology,
12. *See also* Textbooks, Public Administration
Public/Private differences: Bureau of
Municipal Research analysis, 96–
98, 147–148n.31; Morris Cooke
analysis, 75–77; in employment
agencies, 96; Henry Metcalfe
analysis, 29; Dwight Waldo's
analysis of early literature on, 15,
95; Woodrow Wilson analysis
cited in public-administration literature, 29, 30, 75, 141n.21

Redfield, Rep. William, 63
Rockefeller, John D., 91, 145n.3
Roethlisberger, F. J., 81, 113, 114;
views on rate cuts, 115. *See also*
Hawthorne Experiments

Sayre, Wallace, 96
Schelling, Thomas, 69
Schmidt narrative, 39
Scholarship. *See* Arts-Based Model
of Scholarship; Natural-Science
Model of Scholarship
Scientific management, 37–48; and
public-sector responsiveness, 77.
See also Bureau of Municipal Re-
search; Cooke, Morris; Taylor,
Frederick Winslow
Scientific model of scholarship. *See*
Natural Science Model of Scholar-
ship
Self-actualization, 11, 82
Shaiken, Harley, 13–14, 20
Shop Management: publication of, 37.
See also Scientific Management;
Taylor, Frederick Winslow

Shroyer, George, 85
Simon, Herbert, 7, 15; textbook de-
scription of Hawthorne experi-
ments, 113–114
Smith, Merritt Roe, 13
Stevens Institute of Technology, 21,
26
Systematic management, 28–36

Tarbell, Ida, 51–52
Taylor, Emily Winslow, 19
Taylor, Franklin, 19
Taylor, Frederick Winslow: adherents, 50–55; attitude to manual
labor, 20–21, 39–40, 114; American Society of Mechanical Engineers, participation in, 32–36,
52–53; as apprentice, 20–22; background, 19; and Louis Brandeis,
53–55, 56; and civil-service reform, 73, 77–78; and college education, 21; in post-World War II
comparisons to later writers, 11–
12, 18, 54, 111–112, 113–114, 116–
117; and Morris Cooke, 49, 51,
53, 57, 69–70, 73–75, 78, 80, 85,
88–89; as a consultant, 27; and
data collection, 25–26, 38–41; as
a foreman, 24–27; government
efficiency manuscript, 73; idealism
of, 35, 67–69; imitators, 58–63;
and information, 25–26, 38–41;
literary style, 8, 17–18, 40, 49–50,
117–121; management opponents,
34–36, 55–58; and Henry Metcalfe,
28–30, 41; and the National Bureau of Utilities Research, 85; and
Progressive politics, 51–55; and
public-administration public opportunities, 72; and public administration's development as
a discipline, 1; reputation, 1–3;
Schmidt narrative, use of, 39–40,
114; and shop management, 37–
48; and testimony before U.S.